The Golden Age of Sound Comedy

By the Same Author

Four Great Comedians
Focus on Chaplin

The Golden Age of Sound Comedy

Comic Films and Comedians of the Thirties

Donald W. McCaffrey

South Brunswick and New York: A. S. Barnes and Company
London: The Tantivy Press

© 1973 by A. S. Barnes and Co., Inc.
Library of Congress Catalogue Card Number: 78-37814

A. S. Barnes and Co., Inc.
Cranbury, New Jersey 08512

The Tantivy Press
108 New Bond St.
London W1Y OQX, England

Library of Congress Cataloging in Publication Data

McCaffrey, Donald W
    The golden age of sound comedy.

    Bibliography: p.
    1. Comedy films. I. Title.
PN1995.9.C55M32   1973   791.43′090917   78-37814
ISBN 0-498-01048-1

ISBN: 0-498-01048-1 (U.S.A.)
SBN: 90073-064-1 (U.K.)
Printed in the United States of America

Contents

Acknowledgments

Behind the scene, groups, institutions, and many individuals have been of assistance in the creation of *The Golden Age of Sound Comedy*. Once more the Faculty Research Committee of the University of North Dakota has recognised the importance of cinema studies. The Chicago division of Films Incorporated and Elliott Film Company, Minneapolis, have been most helpful with their splendid collections of movies of the Thirties. These rental agencies have given encouragement that shows sensitivity to this type of book. Larry Edmunds Bookshop and Collectors Bookstore in Hollywood, California have also given assistance. Jonathan Levine of New York City has helped greatly with his research, views, and perspective on many films and comedians of the period. Special photographic reproductions by Jerry Olson of Instructional Communications at the University of North Dakota have aided the overall design of this book. And, finally, most important to an author, my wife, Joann, whose perspective has helped me so much before, has shared the creative process once more.

Introduction

The Thirties was the age that witnessed the perfection of the sound motion picture; it was also the Golden Age of Sound Comedy. After an examination of the humorous films created in that period, with the benefit of four decades' hindsight, it can be said that American sound comedy was at its peak during a span of five or six years in the mid-Thirties, a brief but fertile age that ran the gamut of comedy types.

While I was not born early enough to experience the fabulous wealth of humour displayed in the Twenties, some memories of the magnificent Thirties are etched deeply in my mind. In writing this book it has been a pleasure to screen some of the works created during my boyhood. The years have produced a sea change, and some of the films have faded in quality and their ability to stimulate laughter. On the other hand, many of the comedies viewed have taken on a new meaning that could not be grasped by a child in the late Thirties.

To form an accurate account of the sound comedy, I found it necessary to record the soundtracks of many movies. Most of the quoted dialogue has been transcribed directly from a tape of the production. *The Golden Age of Sound Comedy* attempts to show the continuation of several comic traditions and the development of new ones in the Thirties. Unlike the sequels of movies, I am not rehashing my previous work *Four Great Comedians; Chaplin, Lloyd, Keaton, and Langdon*. In a sense I'm merely continuing where the last study stopped. These kings of comedy have their influence in the Thirties, but they do not dominate the scene. Sound changed the rules of the game, and a new art had to be created.

This book focuses on the rise of new talents and an age with a range of comedy form. As in the previous work, I am comparing major comedians. However, by its very nature, the diversification of entertainment offered by several films of the period, make it necessary to examine movies that are not merely products of superior comic actors and actresses. The full spectrum of humour makes this age of comedy fascinating to me and, it is hoped, an experience and enthusiasm for an age will be re-lived through reading this book or experienced vicariously for the first time by the younger reader.

1

Birth Pangs of the Talkies

JUDGE: You're charged here with disorderly conduct. Found makin' violent love to this woman in the park. What have you to say for yourself?
EDDIE: Well, I admit it, Your Honor. I was making love to this woman in the park, but it's perfectly all right—she's my wife. (*He produces a document from his inside coat pocket.*) Why, here's our marriage certificate.
JUDGE: Case dismissed.
(*As Eddie leaves the court, a policeman stops him on the sidewalk in front of the station.*)
POLICEMAN: Say, I'm sorry I arrested you. I didn't know that was your wife.
EDDIE: Neither did I until you put the flashlight in her face. (*He gently nudges the cop with his elbow, grins, and gets into his car.*)

A curiosity today, this short, off-colour scene opened a one-reeler called *Getting a Ticket* and featured the famous Broadway star Eddie Cantor. Released to the public in March 1930, there was little in the work that distinguished it from a vaudeville skit on the stage. With few changes in locale, the cameras were generally static. The camera moved only when Eddie was shown being pursued by a traffic cop immediately after his case for "disorderly conduct" had been dismissed. Eddie then sang a song to the policeman to prove he was the famous actor, Cantor. Odd as it may seem, the comedian didn't dance as he sang "My Wife Is on a Diet." Evidently he was confined by the sound recording restrictions often placed on actors in the formative stage of the talkies.

The labour pains lasted over two and a half years. This slow birth of the sound film obviously wasn't exactly the revolution some historians have called it. By the mid-Thirties the baby had been delivered and most silent screen actors had decided to join the talkies, give up, or face the fact that they were in a new medium that no longer desired their services. Even at this time, however,

not every movie theatre had converted to sound. Silent as well as sound versions of such works as *Showboat* and *Broadway,* unlikely films for this treatment to be sure, were released by Universal in 1929. While *Broadway's* sound version was an all-talkie, *Showboat* retained one of the characteristics of the transitional period—it was a part-dialogue film with some sequences silent and some in sound. The granddaddy of them all established this tradition. Premiering October 6, 1927, the precursor of all musicals and the step that broke the silence, *The Jazz Singer* with Al Jolson, was sprinkled with six recorded songs by the star. Most of the dialogue and the bulk of the development of the film were handled with the old silent screen technique of titles. Comic elements in *The Jazz Singer* were slight; the basic story line was serious, and only a few light touches brought out in song now and then could be called humorous.

Comedy got into the act early in the game. Lee De Forrest, one of the leading scientists in the development of optic sound (sound on film rather than on phonograph discs), filmed and exhibited skits by such famous vaudeville comedians as Weber and Fields, Ben Bernie, George Jessel, and Eddie Cantor—many of these short movies being shown between 1923 and 1926. Kenneth Macgowan in *Behind the Screen* even credits the sound pioneer with the production of the first two-reel sound comedy, *Love's Old Sweet Song,* a work reported to have been created in 1924.

Obviously, no all-dialogue, feature length comedy came into being until 1929. Warner Brothers' 1928 July release, *The Lights of New York,* was a serious work with a dull story and poor acting. The move to comedy in one- and two-reel works had, by this time, however, become a trend. Shorts in the movie industry have always thrived on novelty, and sound was clearly a move that would provide, as Educational Comedies advertised, the "Spice of the Program." Producers in the field, Al Christie and Mack Sennett, by the middle of 1928, were "independents" negotiating contracts to release talkies through larger companies. At this same time Fox Film Corporation, which had concentrated on developing a Fox News series, decided to abandon production of silent two-reel comedies. The whole industry was posed for the big switchover. But it was more cautious than often reported. In 1928 most feature and short producers who attempted to use sound were only half convinced—so they created part-dialogue, music, and sound effect pictures.

Caution and confusion gave birth to some odd hybrids of the old silent screen tradition and the talkies throughout 1929 and 1930. A September 1929 Our Gang two-reeler, *Boxing Gloves,* for example, used sound in close and medium shots, but sometimes displayed long shots without any sound even though kid spectators were screaming loudly for their favourite boy boxer. Many novelty shorts with titles that went something like "Songs of the World," "Melody Parade," etc. were poorly synchronised and employed camera set-ups that did not fit the action.

The deluge came in 1929. Musicals and revues were released by all major companies. And the spark that seemed to fire all of them was the first all-talking (and what some over-enthusiastic public relations man labelled "100% Talking, Singing, and Dancing") musical, *Broadway Melody.* All the *clichés* of the show business success story, the situation of the suave, lecherous, city slicker pursuing the innocent, small town girl, etc., came full blown from M-G-M studios with the production of this picture. Silent film mills had already ground out similar show biz dramas. Sanctified with sound, the hydra-headed monster was to solidify the formula for, it would now seem, the eternity of movie musicals. By critical standards of the age, the picture was a miserable creation, but the novelty of sound made it a success.

Dreary as the basic sentimental plot of *Broadway Melody* was, the comedy was even worse. The stuttering of an agent for the two female protagonists (played by Bessie Love and Anita Page) called "Uncle Jed" provided the bulk of the comedy. For example, at the fade out Bessie, playing the role of a perky, little woman called Hank, spoke of the success they would have on the road with a new show: "It's cream in the can!" Inarticu-

late Jed struggled: "Eh, Eh, Eh (then desperately finished) It's in the can!" Minor comedy bits by a drunken backer of the show and an effeminate costume designer proved equally simple minded humour. Some light comedy developed from the efforts of the leading man (Charles King) to capture the affections of the right girl. Naturally, this type of comedy became one of the major ingredients of a legion of musicals that came to the screen in the Thirties.

With about seven songs and three big production numbers, *Broadway Melody*'s tired plot wasn't helped by the acting. But, as hoary as the situation was even then, it at least had continuity. Many of the pictures that appeared in 1929 after this work didn't even try—they were revues. *Fox Movietone Follies, On with the Show, Gold Diggers of Broadway, Hollywood Revue,* and *Show of Shows* heralded the major studios' entrance into the sound era. Essentially variety shows with all the earmarks of turn of the century vaudeville, such productions are, at best, reflections of light entertainment of that age. A great deal of music and song, a dash of serious drama (even Shakespeare), dances, gaudy production numbers, comedy skits, acrobatics—with the addition of Technicolor in some sequences or the total film—made these pictures unique monstrosities.

Journalistic evaluators of these revues generally had to pick several sketches which appealed or disturbed them—so great was the amount of material. In *Time* magazine of June 10, 1929 the reviewer found the routines of Stepin Fetchit, a black comedian who appeared in many films in the Thirties as the shiftless, slow-witted Negro servant, a contribution to *Fox Movietone Follies* and the singing of Ethel Waters "exciting" in *On with the Show.* But the critic was distressed with attempts to use Technicolor in movies: "The color production in cinemas has not yet been perfected even as well as sound."

Warner Brothers' two important revues of the year were strong, contrasting works. *Gold Diggers* was lacking in name stars that would stand the test of time, but *Show of Shows,* produced late in the year, had Frank Fay and Beatrice Lillie. Minor comedians from the silent screen, Heinie Conklin, Lupino Lane, Ben Turpin, and Lloyd Hamilton, also assisted with humorous sketches. The scene chewing talents of John Barrymore executing a soliloquy from *Richard III,* was probably Warners' attempt to "give class" to the total *potpourri.* With this bit of pretentiousness existed a scene called a

"Military Parade" with three hundred dancing girls and the Pasadena American Legion Fife and Drum Corps. Clearly, the whole production resembled the television presentation "The Ed Sullivan Show." We need not cast stones.

Attempting to develop an even more star-studded cast was *The Hollywood Revue*. M-G-M had contracted silent screen comedians Laurel and Hardy, Buster Keaton, Marie Dressler, and a vaudeville stand-up humourist, Jack Benny, as master of ceremonies. John Gilbert and Norma Shearer appeared in a *Romeo and Juliet* scene—the standard "Balcony Scene," of course. Marion Davies, William Haines, and Lionel Barrymore also made appearances. All of this created the typical revue—no one really had more than a moment of glory as he appeared in a feature picture that would become merely something that happened and not a film that would live among the masterpieces of movie history.

The revue had its greatest vogue in 1929 and 1930, the transitional period. However, it was a *genre* that appeared from time to time throughout the Thirties. With a small range of plot complications, usually something to do with show business, this type of film strung together a series of vaudeville routines or, as stage professionals called it, "turns." Many musicals followed a sketchy, transparent plot line that could place them in this category. "Gold Digger" films appeared in 1933, 1935, and 1938. *Goldwyn Follies* (1938) and the "Big Broadcast" movies all seem to follow the tradition of the variety show. The persistence and the popularity of the revue might explain the disjointed characteristics of so many comedy and musical works of the period. But anyone who is now middle-aged—let's say forty-five to fifty-five—can remember the tenor of the times. During the depression people had few places to go, little to do, lots of time to do nothing much, and little money even if they had the opportunity to do anything. It was a relatively simple age with simple tastes compared to the Seventies. Radio, like the movies, reflected the mass acceptance of assorted, mixed entertainment and an almost benign appreciation of anything that would make the world seem brighter. Most people wanted something light, gay, thrilling, funny—in short, that which entertained. Serious social commentary did exist in this age, but most of it that existed in the movies was very indirect. The Western, the gangster drama, even the historical romance had implicit social messages that often provided day dreams for the average man who asserted his individuality against those forces and people he believed were crushing him. And this was the world of film, as we are now beginning to realise—the place of value reinforcement, of hope, and escape. The comic drama as well as the serious drama served such purposes.

While the average musical on Broadway was not any better than the average movie product of the same *genre*, successful works brought to Hollywood from the stage helped change the whole nature of the films. It became a trend that has lasted to our present day movies. Not only more effective musicals reached the screen, but, most important of all, the talent enlisted became the seed for the flowering of the second golden age of screen comedy. The 1929 movie *Rio Rita*, after an extensive poll of critics by the trade publication *Film Daily*, was rated fourth to *Disraeli*, a work starring the famous actor of the legitimate stage, George Arliss. *Rio Rita* brought a minor comedy team, Bert Wheeler and Robert Woolsey, to the medium. And, fortunately, this same year the Marx Brothers were lured into films when they reproduced for cinema their successful Broadway musical, *Cocoanuts*.

While some critics* seem to dismiss the revue and the musical in the study of the comic film, I see these two types as a key to a more thorough understanding of humour in cinema from the Thirties to our present day. While a "pure" form of comedy drama existed in the Thirties, many of the leading comedians of the time, W. C. Fields, Laurel and Hardy, and the Marx Brothers, were influenced by this type of film entertainment. This was a part of the spectrum of comedy that made the Thirties such an intriguing age of film.

---

*For example, British evaluator Raymond Durgnat in *The Crazy Mirror: Hollywood Comedy and the American Image* dismisses the musical because he sees it as an irregular, arbitrary form.

Warners' Theatre in New York, site of the *première*
of *The Jazz Singer* on October 6, 1927.

Al Jolson and May McAvoy in *The Jazz Singer* (1927).

Cover of sheet music with the plug for the first feature length musical, *Broadway Melody*, released in March of 1929.

Ad for Radio Pictures plugging two 1929 Broadway musical adaptations.

George Renavent (centre) and Bebe Daniels in *Rio Rita* (1929).

M-G-M's *Our Modern Maidens* receives a boast from the cover sketch of Joan Crawford on a song sheet. The film was released in August, 1929.

Ad for Warners' June 1929 production. The first
colour, all-talking revue.

VITAPHONE
recreates

The GOLD DIGGERS of BROADWAY

in 100% NATURAL COLOR

IN TECHNICOLOR

Hear these sparkling song hits: "Tip Toe through the Tulips," "Painting the Clouds with Sunshine," "In a Kitchenette" and "Go to Bed."

Picture a profuse procession of revue spectacle scenes in amazing settings ... superbly staged chorus dancing numbers ... the flashing wit and sparkling songs of Winnie Lightner ... the charm of Nancy Welford ... the astounding dancing of Ann Pennington ... the crooning of Nick Lucas ... love scenes as only Conway Tearle can play them ... a parade of twelve headline players in the leading roles of a story that had New York gasping and giggling for one solid year ... and you have only begun to imagine the treat that is in store for you.

Look for the thrill of a lifetime the day you see "Gold Diggers of Broadway"... And look for the Vitaphone sign when you're looking for talking picture entertainment—always!

Vitaphone is the registered trademark of the Vitaphone Corporation.

You *see* and *hear* Vitaphone *only in* Warner Bros. *and* First National *Pictures*

Warners' September 1929 revue.

Paramount adapted the stage work *Burlesque*, re-titled *The Dance of Life*, in September 1929. From a cover of sheet music.

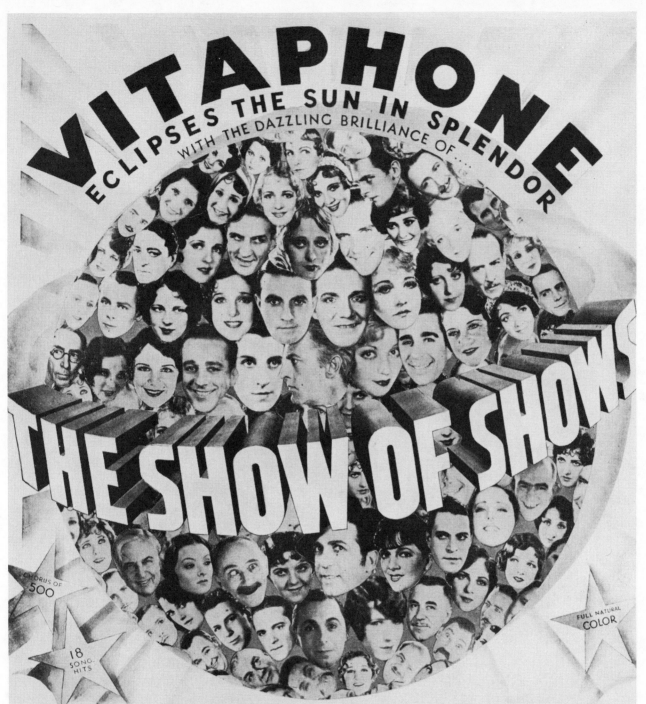

VITAPHONE
ECLIPSES THE SUN IN SPLENDOR
WITH THE DAZZLING BRILLIANCE OF...

THE SHOW OF SHOWS

CHORUS OF 500

18 SONG HITS

FULL NATURAL COLOR

WITH 77 OF THE BRIGHTEST STARS IN HOLLYWOOD'S HEAVEN

Since their first startling introduction of *Vitaphone* Warner Bros. have gradually massed wonder upon wonder—until it seemed that talking picture progress had surely reached its peak.

But now suddenly at a single stride *Vitaphone* comes forward with an achievement so immeasurably superior to any that have gone before, that the history of screen development must be completely rewritten and revised.

"THE SHOW OF SHOWS" is a connoisseur's collection of the supreme examples of almost every form of stage and screen entertainment, each elaborated

beyond the wildest dreams of Broadway or Hollywood.

Only such popularity as *Vitaphone* has attained could provide the resources for assembling the names of John Barrymore, Richard Barthelmess, Beatrice Lillie, Ted Lewis, Georges Carpentier, Irene Bordoni, Dolores Costello, and enough more for 20 average pictures, all on one prodigious program.

And you'll remember as long as you live such sensational features as the Floradora Sextet composed of headline screen stars—the Sister Number with eight sets of celebrated screen-star sisters—the stupendous Lady Luck finale with a chorus of 300 and fifteen specialty "acts" —the Star Curtain on which all the famous favorites in the cast appear simultaneously, framed in one vast fabric!

If you could see only one motion picture this season, that picture should be the "The Show of Shows". Don't dare miss it—for you may never look upon its like again!

A WARNER BROS. & VITAPHONE NATURAL COLOR PICTURE

"Vitaphone" is the registered trade mark of the Vitaphone Corporation
Color scenes by the Technicolor Process

A SWEEPING DEMONSTRATION OF THE SUPREMACY OF VITAPHONE PICTURES, PRODUCED EXCLUSIVELY BY WARNER BROS. AND FIRST NATIONAL

A plug for Warners' most spectacular revue, released
December 1929.

Publicity photo for "Our Gang" during the transitional period. Jackie Cooper, extreme left.

Here it comes!—The hit that made "Tea for Two" a national anthem . . . The smash that shattered all musical romance records in its one-year run on Broadway . . . Brought to you on the screen in all its glory—and more!—More girls—more song-hits— more stars — more stupendous settings than the stage production! . . . . . .

A unique round-the-world romance with Bernice Claire and Alexander Gray— convulsing comedy by Louise Fazenda, Lilyan Tashman, and Lucien Little-field—studded with the most sump-tuous song-and-dance scenes ever filmed, in full COLOR! . . .

Directed by Clarence Badger. From the musical comedy by Frank Mandel, Otto Harbach, Vincent Youmans, Emil Nyitray. . . .

"NO, NO, NANETTE"

A FIRST NATIONAL & VITAPHONE PICTURE

VITAPHONE Picture

"Vitaphone" is the registered trade-mark of The Vitaphone Corporation. Color scenes by Technicolor

First National Pictures

First National's ad for the movie adaptation in 1930 of a popular stage musical.

The potpourri revue continued, still using many stars,
in the 1938 *Goldwyn Follies* as this cover from sheet
music clearly illustrates.

2
Kings in Exile

With the coming of sound the comedy kings of the silent era, Charles Chaplin, Harold Lloyd, Buster Keaton, and Harry Langdon, faced deposition. In only a matter of time they would reign no more. But there was no clear-cut *coup d' état*. Chaplin and Lloyd, like aging dignified monarchs, were never completely dethroned; Keaton and Langdon, having already suffered disfavour, sought to regain their former status. Chaplin's magic seemed to be eternal. Even Lloyd's slick, gag-filled comedies of the Thirties were box-office successes and, in many cases, critically smiled upon—sometimes lauded. But all four of the kings of silence were being replaced by the invading, wise-cracking horde from vaudeville and burlesque. Even those with slight, embryonic grains of comic talent, such as the song and dance men from the stage, were imported to Hollywood to play roles in the flood of musical comedies that poured from the mills between 1929 and the mid-Thirties.

With only two features created in this period to his credit, Chaplin fared better than his rivals of the Twenties. *City Lights* (1931) and *Modern Times* (1936) were not just his only films of the Thirties; they were produced essentially as silent screen comedies in utter defiance of the sound tradition which had been firmly established by the middle of the year 1930. Harold Lloyd, like the eager, adventurous character he portrayed, jumped into sound films with *Welcome Danger* in 1929. Five more films followed: *Feet First* (1930), *Movie Crazy* (1932), *The Cat's Paw* (1934), *The Milky Way* (1936), and *Professor Beware* (1938).

As a forthcoming work by the master comedian, *City Lights* received the attention a year and a half before it was presented that most movies obtain a month before the *première*. Mordaunt Hall

in the July 14, 1929 *New York Times* reported Chaplin's contempt for sound pictures and his desire to make only minor concessions to the tide of productions that was frantically adding music, sound effects, and dialogue. Stubbornly he refused to dub in the sound of closing doors or applause from a crowd. In fact, he wanted no sound effect that had become the staple of most films by mid-1929—even the "part-talking" and "music synchronated" pictures. Sound might be symbolic or used for gag purposes. Interestingly enough, he declared that he would not be adverse to an incidental song, though he did not use it until *Modern Times* in 1936. This meant lyrics and what might seem an illogical concession, since it would indicate the use of dialogue and the human voice. But Chaplin wanted the type of abstraction from reality that silence gave him. To him a song would still be avoiding the motion picture world of chatter which he found so offensive.

At a gala *première* in New York February 6, 1931, the little tramp once more stole the hearts of the fans and the critics. Without a doubt, *City Lights* remains as one of the greatest works by Chaplin. A brilliant, ironic little scene opened the picture. A veiled monument was shown as a title flashed: "To the people of the city we donate this monument" and the soundtrack, using a jabbering saxophone, imitated the senseless gabble of dedicatory speeches—and possibly revealed Chaplin's disparaging attitude toward the sound film. With the unveiling of huge, granite, Amazon-Roman women, the audience at the dedication became appalled by the sight of the little tramp asleep on the lap of one of the figures. Struggling to get down from the statue when a policeman threatened him, Charlie got his pants caught on the sword of a big boned goddess. Free from this obstacle, he laboured to tidy himself by leaning over to tie his shoe. His nose pressed close to the thumb of another statue so that he seemed to be making some comment on the whole affair. Then he jauntily tipped his hat and left.

While this short, introductory scene revealed the well-established facets of Chaplin's character, what followed gave a new dimension to the little tramp. More of a dandy than in previous pictures, he viewed a nude statue of a woman in a store window with the air of a connoisseur of art. His attitudes when he fell in love with a blind girl showed him in a new light. True, much of the best comedy in such works as *The Gold Rush* (1925) and *The Circus* (1928) indicated that he had previously endowed the little outcast with attempted dignity and pretence. But there was a new dash and charm in the character that had not been fully developed until *City Lights*.

The plotting of this movie was a cut about the comedian's feature films; nevertheless, it remained episodic—almost a patch and paste job at times— and held together more through the force of Chaplin's intriguing character and superb acting. One of the best sequences in the picture was the prize fight. Refurbished gags and routines from such early works as the two reeler, *The Knockout* (1914), in which Chaplin played a referee, and *The Champion* (1915) with the comedian as the underdog prize fighter, helped sell the comedy in this portion of the picture. Pantomimed boxing that came closer to comic ballet made it a highlight for the critics of the time.

Not noted for effective verbal gags, Chaplin produced a few in *City Lights* that were outstanding. Seated next to a drunken millionaire in a madly careening automobile after a night on the town, the little tramp remarked (through the use of a title, of course): "Be careful how you drive." His friend asked, "Am I driving?" Less drunk than the millionaire, Charlie frantically clutched the wheel of the car to gain control.

Undeniably gifted, Chaplin proved that regardless of the universal change to sound, a person with enough talent could buck the system. He was an incurable rebel and romantic. In a press release before *City Lights* premiered (See *New York Times,* January 25, 1931, section 8, page 6), he stated that the silent film had been "temporarily pushed aside in the hysteria attending the introduction of speech." He maintained the view that silent films would experience a revival and was

even audacious enough to write that the sound film was an addition to the art, "not a substitute."

Always the darling of the New York critics, Chaplin was hailed with kudos for his presentation of *City Lights*. Critics such as Richard Watts, Jr., Mordaunt Hall, and Thornton Delehanty were ecstatic. It did not bother them that their favourite comedian still made silent pictures. In fact, nearly forty years later, it is possible for modern day critics to say it was better that he did stay with the older tradition, for some believe *City Lights* to be his greatest film. He may not have been able to make the transition to sound.

I believe Theodore Huff in his splendid work, *Charlie Chaplin,* overstates his case when he calls *City Lights* one of the comedian's most original story ideas with "the accent as much on the love story as on the humor; and its prevailing attitude of sharp irony." The love story is not particularly outstanding or original; Harry Langdon in the 1926 *The Strong Man* had his little fellow fall in love with a blind girl. Chaplin does, however, bring the story to a highly effective end, a tender meeting between the little tramp and the girl who has been cured of her blindness. No longer does Charlie appear to her as the man of her dreams—merely a shabby, pathetic, small man. Charlie's realisation of her thoughts provides one of the great moments of all screen drama. A scene that might have been maudlin is handled with the restraint and skill of a pantomime that has not been matched.

What Huff calls irony was best developed by the on and off relationship of the little tramp with a millionaire. In the world of drunken revelry the millionaire slobberingly embraces Charlie and hits all the best night clubs with him; in the cold light of dawn he becomes a sober, stuffed-shirt who abhors the sight of the little fellow. This element of the plot is well executed and has some of the strongest comedy.

Chaplin's second work of the Thirties, *Modern Times,* opened in New York on February 5, 1936 with many notables attending: Will Hays, Adolph Zukor, Harry Warner, Lee Shubert, Lillian Hellman, Lord and Lady Plunkett, Edward G. Robinson, Burns and Allen, Douglas Fairbanks (and his son), Ginger Rogers, Anna May Wong, Consuelo Vanderbilt, Mrs. Vincent Astor, Miss Elsa Maxwell, and of course, all the critics.

Chaplin could do no wrong. Essentially he presented everyone with a silent picture at a time when people had begun to forget the whole tradition. Sight or pantomime comedy remained a part of most comedy films—a routine or a scene or two—but here was a total "silent" work that was very successful—that stayed in the world of yesterday.

Modern Times was the comedian's last great work—or, at least, the last great work that featured a full blown version of the little tramp. While some evaluators will not agree, I believe it was his first film to attempt direct social commentary of a sort. But Chaplin was not an Aristophanes, Molière, or Shaw. With more interviews and statements to the press than previously, a great deal of conjecture developed regarding *Modern Times*'s intentions of satirising American industry. To make things even more speculative, Chaplin treated the head of the Russian film production, B. Z. Shumiatsky, to a preview of several scenes of the picture when he visited Hollywood. *Pravda*, of course, ballooned what had been seen out of all proportion by declaring that the film was "filled with fearful accusation." (See *New York Times*, September 29, 1935, section 10, page 4.)

When the film opened in February 1936, New York critics found that it was a burlesque—satire it was not. The tone, strength, penetration, and quality of the humour placed it on this plane. Chaplin, it should be realised, never had pretensions that it would be a masterpiece of social comment; he insisted that he was an entertainer and not an evaluator of society who lectured to his public. Film critic Frank S. Nugent of the *Times* was pleased that the work was not loaded with "social messages." Theatre reviewer Brooks Atkinson with the grace of his colleague, Nugent, turned from stage to screen in an elaborate article entitled "Beloved Vagabond" to write that if *Modern Times* could be taken "as social comment, it is plain that he [Chaplin] has hardly passed his entrance examination, his comment is so trivial." However, Atkinson declared: "As an actor he has never been more brilliant."

This 1936 work revealed the comedian's continuance of the silent screen tradition and marked a new height in his acting skills. As Robert Payne observed in *The Great God Pan*, *Modern Times* presented the best and the worst of Chaplin. It had great sequences, splendid comic routines, but lacked the overall unity of such works as *City Lights* and *The Gold Rush*.

What may have achieved unity—a strong, central comic idea—is revealed in the first sequence of the picture. This, however, is not pursued fur-

ther. A twenty minute episode in an eighty-five minute film, this portion shows Chaplin shooting his bolt after only a fourth of the work had developed. It is a deftly edited sequence with over a hundred shots and a variety of shots seldom seen in a Chaplin work. It also features a series of sound effects and vocal elements which are compromises with the talking picture which the comedian allowed in his film. A sound of a factory whistle, a bell to signal central control to step up production, sounds from an automatic feeding machine (to keep workers productive during normal lunch periods), explosions from large dynamos shorting out when the wrong switches are pulled, and a siren of an ambulance to take away the berserk little tramp when he suffered a nervous breakdown on the assembly line are some of the sound effects which Chaplin incorporated. Not new to the sound or silent medium, of course, was the introduction of a symbolic music score—most significantly used when the speed of the assembly line machinery was increased and when the little fellow's brain cracked under the strain. More of a compromise was produced, however, with the use of the closed-circuit television orders of the plant owner in his Big Brother reprimand of Charlie, who took too long a break in the factory lavatory. Also, the boss was given a sales talk on the automatic feeding machine via a phonographic recording.

All these elements show that the comedian was grudgingly accepting the new medium; but, it should be noted, all of the sounds mentioned above were related to the mechanical—which was the object of his lampoon. Furthermore, in the last five minutes of *Modern Times* he fulfils an earlier musing that he would not be adverse to employing an incidental song. As if still in defiance of a medium that had supplanted his art, he sang in a curious jabberwacky of his own creation to the tune of a Spanish fandango. The words were a curious pseudo Spanish, Italian, and French that only made sense when Chaplin's pantomiming of the little story was seen. He was highly skilled in this singing and dancing, and an evaluator of today can only arrive at a vague conjecture that the famous comedian might have produced successful sound comedies if he had wholeheartedly embraced the medium in 1929.

Modern Times, in my view, was the last Chaplin film that truly revealed his genius. With all its faults the film, screened today, becomes a fascinating Chaplin sampler—a series of comic routines refurbished from the past, touches of his pathos, and moments of great comic gaiety. Had Chaplin maintained the strength of the first factory sequence with minor switches of more delicate humorous tones to provide shading, he would have produced a brilliant film that might have excelled his two masterpieces, *The Gold Rush* and *City Lights*. His acting, by this time, was at its peak of maturity and perfection.

The comedian's fight against the obvious permanent status of the sound motion picture ended soon after *Modern Times*. It never was clear why he changed his mind, but he evidently didn't wish to announce his retreat from such a strong stand. Max Eastman reported that about 1938 he found the artist of comedy immersed in script writing (*Great Companions*, p. 227). Chaplin claimed that he might not talk himself but would direct Paulette Goddard in a film. Two years later he featured himself in a picture, *The Great Dictator*, and the world heard him talk for the first time. All sound techniques were incorporated, and he employed the sound comedy films standard practice of relying on other comedians, Jack Oakie, Reginald Gardiner, and Billy Gilbert, to assist him in sustaining the total work. Not that he had previously avoided using other actors in major roles; but, he was bringing established sound film comedians into his company for the picture. In the past he had tended to pick relatively unknown comedians to play opposite him. The script had all the earmarks of a sound comedy but not many of its virtues. Some moments are worthy of the master, containing the grain of the comedian's fading glory. He remained most effective when he employed the old pantomime approach to his material. There were such routines as the globe dance scene which revealed Hynkel (a travesty on the most infamous dictator of our time, Hitler) juggling the world like a ball. The weakest scene was the last. A speech of good will to mankind comes from the little barber who has become a substitute for the dictator after being mistaken for Hynkel. The speech was out of character, poorly motivated, and dealt essentially in sophomore polemics that proved Chaplin should have left political philosophy to politicians and professors.

Walter Kerr put his finger on the transformation of Chaplin's working method when he stated that the comedian had made a "hopeless capitulation to words" in a medium that stressed the visual ("The Lineage of *Limelight*," *Theatre Arts*, No-

vember 1952, pp. 73-75). Kerr recapped some of the comedian's great moments in past films and found a profundity in the actor's visual presentation—the "acting out" of the emotion and the idea. He concluded: "A profound clown—the greatest, most beloved we have—is seeking a second reputation as a sage. It is not likely to equal the first." By the end of the Thirties the master of comedy had placed himself in exile; critics were no longer bowing graciously even to his faults. From then on he would receive mixed reviews with such works as *Monsieur Verdoux* (1947) and *Limelight* (1952).

* * *

In his five successful features in the Thirties, Harold Lloyd never took to the lectern. While his characters and plots often burlesqued the American code of the striving young man who achieves his goals of money and the girl, the lightness of his spoof never allowed for satirical thrusts or preaching. He, more than any other comedian, was able to blend the old tradition with the new and make effective movies.

While he adapted well to vocal comedy, Lloyd's best moments in his sound films were visual. *Movie Crazy* (1932) was probably the most effective picture of the five he made in the Thirties. The 1962 omnibus of his work, *Harold Lloyd's World of Comedy*, allowed the public of today to see a portion of this film. His skill in handling a whole series of gags that develop from one situation was illustrated in the magician coat sequence. In the men's room he accidentally puts on a magician's suit coat and gets involved in a whole chain of embarrassing situations as a result of the error. It was a new approach to comic confusion, similar to the unraveling of his coat in an elaborate episode in *The Freshman* (1926). In the silent screen version of this type of gag, Harold suffered under the stress of a strained social situation; the sound film has embarrassments rain on him and those with whom he comes into contact. A lapel flower sprayed water in the face of his boss's wife as he danced with her. When a white rabbit squirmed from one of the concealed pockets, Harold placed the creature under a large dish cover. A drunk naturally received quite a shock as he saw the live rabbit jump from the plate. A wide variety of such unintentional magic tricks, including mice and chicken eggs coming from the coat, created an entertaining series of comic social situations.

Mordaunt Hall of the *New York Times* observed in his review of September 25, 1932 that the picture "hardly benefits by sound. It is essentially the old silent school technique . . ." And that was probably why it now can be said to be one of Lloyd's best films of the Thirties. Like Chaplin, the silent film was his medium, and when he used more visual than verbal gags, his work was at its highest level. Other scenes in the film revealed memorable moments that are gems of sight comedy. Lloyd's acting skills were especially effective in his bungled attempt to help a young woman (played by Constance Cummings) to get the top of a convertible car up during a rain storm. One end or the other of the top refused to remain fastened until Harold reduced the mechanism to a worthless piece of junk.* In the same scene he also got his shoe caught and pulled off; a clever sight was created as the shoe floated along in the gutter, with Harold executing a wild, one-legged hop in pursuit of his shoe. A 1950 reissue of *Movie Crazy* in London and America illustrated to critics that the comedian's charm and comic skills still held the audience and created a lot of laughter. While it was not always realised by evaluators of Lloyd's work, the comedian succeeded, not merely through the development of a variety of rapid-fire, visual gags, but also by creating a strong comic character. His acting flair made him second to Chaplin by popular acclaim.

When Lloyd first plunged into sound pictures, he tried to make a sharper switch to the new tradition. In *Welcome Danger* (1929), made as a silent film with a large portion re-shot to add sound, he incorporated a humorous lecture on the petunia. In one short scene he used a dark screen effectively, with the dialogue carrying all the comedy.

The comedian's ability to blend the old tradition and the new became more obvious with *Feet First* (1930). He refurbished the "thrill comedy" of three of his short works and *Safety Last* (1923), developing the climactic sequence in a similar fashion by having his comic protagonist caught on the side of a skyscraper and encountering many obstacles as he tries to get to safety. This part of the picture brought the strongest laughs, and while some critics, such as Mordaunt Hall, saw it as a work too similar in content to *Safety Last*, evaluator Nelson Garringer in the August-September 1962 issue of *Films in Review* observed that

the 1930 work was original since it did not repeat any of the gags of its silent screen precursor.

By 1934, Lloyd's tendency to change even more with the sound medium was evident. With *The Cat's Paw* the comedian and his director, Sam Taylor, decided to make the film the "new way"* instead of the "old way." By this decision, which was made by drawing a slip of paper from a hat, they did not labour with a staff of gagmen to develop each sequence. Instead, they stuck with the original scenario created from a Clarence Budington Kelland story. As a result the film avoided the gag-packing approach to film story development which some critics had not found appealing. Reviewers were favourably disposed to *The Cat's Paw* and indicated that they liked the new style because the old slapstick intrigue no longer was as effective. It should be realised that by the mid-Thirties there was a trend toward more genteel forms of comedy. Sophisticated and musical comedy introduced lighter, romantic intrigues that did not focus as much on farcical, slapstick situations. But the older approach kept persisting—even in the sophisticated comedy—which inclined evaluators to label it "screwball" comedy since it sometimes employed wacky situations and the devil-may-care actions of characters.

Lloyd was never, to the end of his life, sure that the drawing of the slip of paper from the hat that said "new way" was the right move. He wondered if he might have made a funnier picture if *The Cat's Paw* had been made the "old way."

Lloyd developed his comedies with more assistance from supporting comedians—a feature of the sound film that differed from the old tradition. Character actors, the staple (and one of the worthy characteristics) of films in the Thirties, assisted the total humorous story line. George Barbier and Nat Pendleton were given strong roles in *The Cat's Paw*. Lloyd's 1936 feature, *The Milky Way*, used Barbier again; also, Adolphe Menjou and Lionel Stander enhanced the story greatly with their characterisations.

Three scenarists, Grover Jones, Frank Butler, and Richard Connell developed an effective story for *The Milky Way*—a work that was remade in 1946 under the title *The Kid from Brooklyn* starring Danny Kaye. The 1936 version also had the capable direction of Leo McCarey, who

---

*In a June 1965 interview with Lloyd, I learned from him that some of the struggling with the car top was not planned—he found it more stubborn than anticipated. Thus, in the silent days, unforeseen difficulties helped a comedy scene.

Time magazine of August 27, 1934, p. 42 and William Cahn's *Harold Lloyd's World of Comedy*, p. 160 gave accounts of this new approach.

handled *Duck Soup* (1933) and *Ruggles of Red Gap* (1936), to help mold the movie into a success. Reviewers lauded the film and diverse publications such as *Literary Review, Time, New Republic,* and *New York Times* reported the work to be one of the strongest comedies of that year.

Although Lloyd believed his last two comedies, *Professor Beware* (1938) and *Mad Wednesday* (1947), were not of the same high quality as earlier works, there are portions in both films that make them enjoyable. *Professor Beware* employs the talent of Lionel Stander, Raymond Walburn, and William Frawley, three excellent character comedians. There are times when Lloyd even seems to play straight man for them. This is especially true of some of the verbal humour. As an archaeologist fleeing from the police, Harold meets two bums (Stander and Walburn) on a freight train. He tells Stander that he is going to Egypt to explore tombs. The tough face wrinkles in disgust, and with the indignant, gravel voice that became well-known, he growls, "I've traveled with many a stinker, but I draw the line at ghouls." Harold also tells him how he feels toward a "good woman"—that she made him happy in an unusual way—". . . still isn't just a woman. She's something else!" To this remark Stander grunts, "A female impersonator?"

However, the most effective portions of the picture are more often visual, not verbal. Even as his glory as a comedy king faded, Lloyd handled beautifully the struggle with a drunken motion picture talent scout, played by William Frawley. In this scene he is trying to exchange clothes with the lush in the back seat of a car. A spectacular race along the top of a freight train to avoid being knocked off or Lloyd's being suffocated by fumes from a low clearance tunnel provided some of the "thrill comedy" that made him famous. The comedian also refurbished an old gag from his 1920 two-reeler, *Get Out and Get Under.* To escape cops in a chase sequence he drives his car into a tent; as he flees when his hideout is discovered, he takes the tent with him—so it appears that a mobile tent is travelling by itself along a road.* Furthermore, Lloyd employed an elaborate chase and fight sequence that lasted over twenty minutes for the climax of his picture—a portion of the work was jammed with visual gags. The final eight minutes is an orgy of men fighting. It is a master-piece of speed and wild movements with over 122 shots used by editor Duncan Mansfield to develop a fascinating finish for the picture.

Had Lloyd been satisfied with *Professor Beware,* he might have continued with an output of a picture every other year. Some of the old spark was still in his portrayal of the archaeologist, but the overall picture had the taint of the Hollywood movie mills of the Thirties. He retired as a star with only occasional work as a producer for RKO in 1941 and 1942. Howard Hughes and director Preston Sturges urged him to return as a leading comic in 1947 for a film called *The Sin of Harold Diddlebock* and re-titled *Mad Wednesday.* Once more the old flair of Lloyd helped the picture, but as a whole it was not one of his best. He believed that the first third of the film had progressed with strong potential but felt the rest of the work went downhill. Fortunately, Lloyd threw in the towel when he realised that the system was no longer one that created or sustained kings of comedy. He retired with at least a respectable film. Some of the last works of other major comedians reveal that they didn't know when to retire. The last works of the Marx Brothers, W. C. Fields, Laurel and Hardy—even Chaplin, are pathetic shadows of their best movies.

Buster Keaton's first starring sound picture, *Free and Easy,* a 1930 M-G-M production, was a popular work, but by modern standards it can be called a dull and dreary affair. Only moments in the picture reflect the former greatness of the comedian. Evidently, he was forced into the type of film that had become the staple of the transitional period. It reflected the worst aspects of a production that turned to "show biz" and musical comedy plot material to satisfy box-office demands.

Buster Keaton adapted surprisingly well to the demands of musical comedy in several song and dance routines toward the end of *Free and Easy.* But there was little in the rest of the work to develop his reputation in sound films. Verbal gags were banal—only an occasional sight gag indicated that Keaton had talked his writers and director into developing one of his own routines. In short, he was being submerged in the new medium as another actor, not a master of comedy. To complete the disaster, he seemed awkward in the handling of his dialogue. Granted, the lines given to him would hardly assist anyone. At best he executed some second rate vaudeville turns with enough skill to show he still was a contender.

Today *Free and Easy* is a curiosity piece for film

---

*Some of this sequence appeared in *Harold Lloyd's Wonderful World of Comedy* in 1962.

historians and fans with nostalgia for the "good old days" which gives them behind-the-stage glimpses of movie-makers of the time. Buster gets involved in three film productions, by accident or design, with David Burton, Lionel Barrymore, and Fred Niblo playing roles as directors—professions at which they were currently engaged. While a variety of film styles are depicted in these play-within-a-play scenes, the overall focus gravitates to the production of a filmed musical—a very wooden creation that illustrates how stupid the musical-variety film could be in this transitional period of 1929/30.

Critics did not view Keaton's sound pictures with the respect often given to a fading star. While biographer Rudi Blesh now rates *Doughboys* (1930) as one of his better pictures (a result, Blesh claims, of Keaton's having more control over his material), there is no evidence that critics at the time found it worthy of his past efforts. Mordaunt Hall classified most of his sound films as inferior Keaton; he found some of the farcical incidents well done but saw the story line and the gags as a product of poor writing. Even with more control of his films (he has a producer's credit for *Doughboys*), Keaton was fading.

By 1933 it looked as if a pairing with Jimmy Durante might help Keaton make the transition to sound pictures. A look at *What! No Beer?*, produced that year, can illustrate why he had difficulty making a successful comeback. Supposedly, the two comedians were working as a team. Jimmy, however, seems to have had a role that often pushed the silent screen comedy king into the background. This lad with the Cyrano de Bergerac profile played his scenes with vigour—the manic strength of his thrusting character dominated and helped move *What! No Beer?* into the category of an above average comedy. The two comedians reflected the attempted blend of comedy in the movie—Keaton adhered to the old tradition and Durante to the new. As a result, the film would seem to support the comeback of Keaton. Many of the better comedies of the time had such a combination. But the new comedy won the day —it seemed to carry the whole work. The best lines are delivered by Durante. Urging Buster (who plays "Elmer Butts"—a name he favoured in sound films) to invest $10,000 in a brewery just as prohibition is about to be repealed, Jimmy shouts his malapropisms to the heavens: "A hundred-twenty million cracked lips are straining at the *leach*. Where's your *patronism*? Here's a chance

to do something for your country." Furthermore, Jimmy, with a headstrong will, takes the most significant action in the picture. Such moves generally get the two protagonists into comic hot water. Only at the end of the picture does Buster get a bright idea which wraps up the whole plot. Since their brewery is threatened with a police raid, he advertises free beer to the townspeople to drink up the evidence.

What! No Beer? seems more a Durante movie than a Keaton movie. But when visual comedy predominates, Buster has a heyday. Driving a huge truck loaded with barrels of beer up a steep hill, he is forced to stop the vehicle to fix a flat tyre. Struggling to get a jack for the operation, Buster loosens some boards that hold the barrels. A delightful bit of mayhem develops as we see the old frozen-faced Buster dashing from a sea of rolling barrels just as gangsters stage a raid on his truck. The little man artfully dodges the bouncing, erratic missiles while the highjackers are mowed down. Similar to an episode from the silent screen, it is a delight that only lasts a few minutes—a portion that might have been expanded twice or three times if it had been created in the Twenties.

Only two years after this feature the comedian was reduced to shorts for Educational Pictures. His career had come full circle—he was back where he started twenty years previously. He was a has-been working in Hollywood as a comedian who would do an occasional bit in a feature or a string of low budget two-reelers. In the late Fifties he made a comeback of sorts in television and the movies. But Keaton was patronised and treated like a side-show freak; never again was he able to control the creative process of a feature length work.

Harry Langdon suffered a similar fate. He had a briefer reign as a comedy king of the silent age— only about two years, 1925 to 1927, but he created three excellent features, *Tramp, Tramp, Tramp* and *The Strong Man* in 1926 and *Long Pants* in 1927, plus several effective shorter works. When he tried to direct his own pictures, however, he failed. Three of his features in the late Twenties were neither critical nor popular successes, and he lost his footing as one of the leading comedians.

After a brief, successful return to M-G-M released sound shorts in 1929 and 1930, he starred in the 1930 *A Soldier's Plaything*. It received only slight attention from the critics of the time. Later the same year, Mordaunt Hall complained that

Langdon's *See America Thirst* suffered from a poor script. Much of the comic material seemed too fast and farcical for the comedian's low-keyed style. Also, Slim Summerville, fresh from the highly successful, best picture of the year, *All Quiet on the Western Front,* seemed to have grasped the sound motion picture style of comedy even though he had been schooled in the broadest type of slapstick as one of Mack Sennett's Keystone Cops. He appeared to be more at home in his role and could make more from the inadequate dialogue of the script than Langdon could.

Forced to return to two-reelers, Langdon made a few amusing shorts for M-G-M and then turned to Educational Pictures, a haven for old comedians and novices that would be the stars of the late Thirties and Forties. The unsuccessful *Hallelujah, I'm a Bum* starring Al Jolson only assured his continuance in two-reelers and bit parts. This 1933 feature showed some indications that Langdon might make a comeback as a comic supporting actor—one who might again achieve star status. But the total work was a failure. Jolson himself seems to have lost the steam and charm of the history-making *Jazz Singer* of 1927. The Rodgers and Hart "rhythmic dialogue" seemed out of place in the pseudo-realistic world of the Hollywood sound stage and gave, in some of the portions of the picture, a warmed-over Broadway tone to the total work. Langdon had a few moments when the old tramp-clown figure sprang to life. But he seemed out of place when trading dialogue with the glib-talking Al Jolson; he even struggled valiantly with a couple of production numbers, but his vaudeville background had trained him more for "dumb" acts—sight gag routines that he seemed to control more effectively in his two-reelers.

All four comedy kings were in exile by the end of the Thirties. They had seen their day. It was not without a considerable amount of influence, however. As they faded into the wings to watch others taking over, they left a vital legacy of visual comedy that will live on. While some may say these comedians did not change with the times, I believe they had reached their peak in an age where they exercised a free film form—almost an improvisational, fresh approach to their material. Like the *commedia dell' arte* players of centuries before, they did their best work with a simple production. Elaborate, well-equipped and controlled sound stages actually confined them. And like all artists with strong creative spirits, they burned themselves out. While the little tramp-clowns, struggling boobs, and social outcasts they created seem to live eternally in the world of silence, the creators of the best comedies of the Twenties had to move from the scene and let others carry on.

In the silent screen days, Charles Chaplin's publicity pose, *circa* 1915.

The wacky situation for which he is best remembered
—Harold Lloyd in *Safety Last* (1923).

As a movie projectionist Buster Keaton encountered difficulties in *Sherlock, Jr.* (1924).

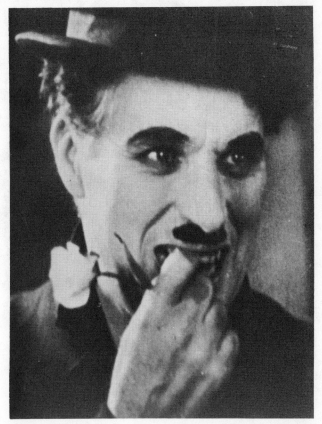

The famous close-up of the Little Tramp in the last scene of *City Lights* (1931).

A Keaton-like stance by Harry Langdon in his three-reel *Soldier Man* (1926).

Going insane on the assembly line in *Modern Times* (1936).

Defying authority in *Modern Times*.

Preparing for a song and dance routine in *Modern Times*.

Chaplin, as Hynkel disagrees with his minister, Gar-
bitsch (Henry Daniell), in *The Great Dictator* (1940).

In *The Great Dictator* the egocentric Hynkel poses
for artists.

The barber in disguise goes to the platform to give
the final speech in place of Hynkel in *The Great
Dictator*.

Chaplin in the role of a dandy in *Monsieur Verdoux* (1947) with Martha Raye.

Almira Sessions, as Lena, begins to recognise the "blue beard" in *Monsieur Verdoux*.

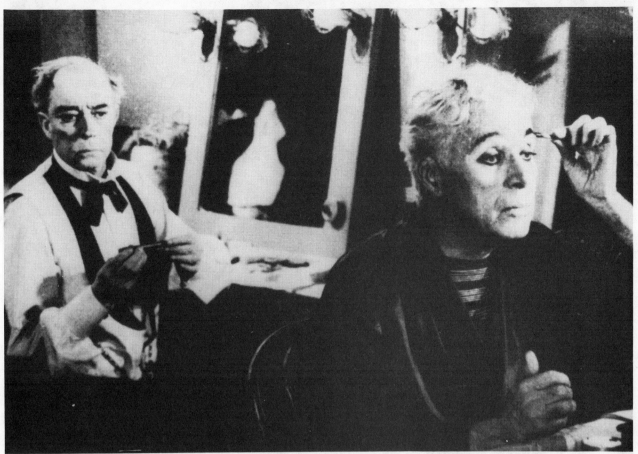

Buster Keaton performs as a colleague in *Limelight* (1952).

With Claire Bloom in *Limelight*.

Harold Lloyd's second talkie, *Feet First* (1930), shows the comedian's use of embarrassment to produce humour.

In *Feet First*, Lloyd as a hapless shoe salesman.

A magician's coat causes strange objects to drop in
his hand in Lloyd's best sound work, Movie Crazy
(1932).

At forty-six, Lloyd had a youthful appearance in *Professor Beware* (1938).

In *Professor Beware* the girl (Phyllis Welch) doesn't realise the man she seeks is just around the gas pump.

In his last film, *Mad Wednesday* (1946), Lloyd has a pet lion and a girl (Frances Ramsden).

Keaton dances in movies for the first time in his first starring role in a talkie, *Free and Easy* (1930).

As Elmer Butts in *What! No Beer?* (1933) Keaton
is dragged away for disturbing a speaker.

Jimmy Durante, as Jimmy Potts, and Elmer cause problems to develop in *What! No Beer?* when they vote against prohibition too enthusiastically.

Posed shot of Harry Langdon for his comic character in *Hallelujah, I'm a Bum* (1933).

Gilbert Roland duels with Buster Keaton as Durante looks on, disturbed about the outcome, in *The Passionate Plumber* (1932).

Al Jolson and Langdon in *Hallelujah, I'm a Bum.*

3

Much Ado about Show Biz: The Musical

"Naughty, gaudy, bawdy," a phrase from the lyrics of a song describing life on 42nd Street in New York indicated some of the characteristics of the 1933 musical. At the beginning of this year the film *42nd Street* was a box-office hit and, in typical Hollywood fashion, a series of similar creations was ground out—a series that mirrored a similar, fevered activity during the transition to sound in 1929. Musicals and variety shows were being produced in the ensuing years but their course ran from a waterfall to a trickle.

What motivated the revitalisation of the genre in the year 1933 might have been the popularity of *42nd Street*. The fact that such films were earthy —gaudy and somewhat "naughty" and "bawdy"— might be a reason for the success. Also, Warner Brothers' elaborate coast to coast pre-release promotion of *42nd Street,* using many stars from the studios such as Laura La Plante, Bette Davis, and Preston Foster at whistle stop appearances on the train labelled the "42nd Street Special," might have created enough interest to provide a market for such films. The most important cause of the renaissance could best be linked to the growing sophistication of the cinematic art that had been achieved since 1929. True, the old ingredients were still ingrained in the basic story line. *42nd Street,* like most musicals, had a light, thin, simple-minded plot line showing colourful, energetic theatre people struggling to create a successful stage production. The product was, at times, as frothy as French confectionery and, at other times, as subtle as Tschaikowsky's "1812 Overture." Director Lloyd Bacon helped whip the whole mess into an appealing dish. Most important of all to the general public were the efforts of Busby Berkeley. With a grandiose flair that departed from the restrictions of the Broadway theatre, he created

gargantuan production numbers that awed the senses of the depression audiences. Even reviewers for *Literary Digest* and *Time* were so impressed with such sequences of the film that they could write on little else.

A view of the total work today reveals many other aspects about *42nd Street* apart from the three spectacular production numbers. There is an earthiness in some of the *risqué* humour that gives this musical and others of the period a distinction. One of the most interesting sequences is the drunken brawl of the cast members of a show called *Pretty Lady*. Such cavorting in a hotel probably pushed sensitive moralists, and especially the Catholic Legion of Decency, into a moral rearmament movement that pressured the Hays Office into a corner. Sexual gags and frankness in depicting the "swinging" life of those in show business abound in the film. Ginger Rogers appears in a bit part of a chorus girl called by her colleagues "Anytime Annie." As she arrives at try-outs, a man declares: "Not Anytime Annie? Who could forget her? She only said 'no' once and then she didn't hear the question." Even more blunt (and what some may call tasteless) humour develops when a chorus girl (Ruby Keeler) is being coached by one of the male dancers. Asked by the director (Warner Baxter) why the two are rehearsing with such dedication, the young man cannot finish his sentence to explain, "I was just tryin' to make her . . ." when another member of the company interrupts with a cut-down: "Trying to make her is right."

Such blatant humour was soon to go underground and be replaced by the more devious *double entendre*. The pressure on the Hays Office that led to the production code of 1934 would not allow direct, sexual comedy. But some of this type of humour would continue in the lyrics of songs throughout the period. One of *42nd Street*'s big production numbers, "Shuffle Off to Buffalo" set the tone and established the standard for songs that teased newlyweds on their wedding night—a type of humour permitted in a large segment of our society in all periods and carried down from the past, evidently because the sexuality of the couple received the sanctions of the church or law. With the teasing amusement of the lyrics there was a cynicism regarding marriage, expressed by a girl trio in a train berth who sang: "When she knows as much as we know, she'll be off to Reno . . ." They even suggested that the union has been by shotgun marriage: "I bet that she's the farmer's daughter and he's the well-known travelling man . . ." Obviously, the sharp edge of the lyrics was muted by the gaiety of the tune. Throughout the Thirties and into the Forties lyrics seemed to retain some of this kind of sexual joke and cynicism—a type that jabbed lightly the sentimental taboos of society.

The production numbers of *42nd Street* that attracted so much attention in 1933 and spurred the whole *genre* on to a revival as an effective, popular film entertainment are difficult to describe because they are so complicated. Busby Berkeley's earlier effort, a vehicle for Eddie Cantor called *Palmy Days* (1931), was little more than weak, feminine, military drills—as routine as the two-dimensional line-up of females in the old-fashioned stage revue. By 1933 the dance director's imagination had flourished; his conception of his art moved away from Broadway and entered the cinema world. Three elaborate production numbers in *42nd Street* using the songs "Shuffle Off to Buffalo," "Young and Healthy," and "42nd Street," were placed at the end of the film to provide a climactic sequence that was not story oriented but provided an orgy of sight and sound. Each offered comic elements: "Young and Healthy" was a lighter number with a gaiety that celebrated the charms of American womanhood, while the other two employed a sharper, anti-sentimental spirit of humour. Progressively, each dance-drama and song routine became more cinematic. Rapid editing of many different shots and angles of view plus camera movement created a world of musical comedy that was flashy and fantastic. The fairy tale world for adults was created as Dick Powell urged a huge chorus of girls to "stay young and healthy," and the camera soared in many overhead shots of the women on turntables—their attire, their legs, and bodies produced geometric patterns that were novel and pleasing to the eye. The song "42nd Street" was the culmination of the visual effects. Ruby Keeler opened with lyrics to this song that describes the variety of life and people in the streets of New York. Berkeley moved his actors in—prostitutes, bums, midgets; and a ballet-like rape, a shooting, and a knifing were witnessed. Such violence may seem to some to be inappropriate as the subject for a light, essentially gay, musical production number, but Berkeley had a taste that occasionally went to such bizarre subjects. His most elaborate number, "Lullaby of Broadway" in *Gold Diggers of 1935* ended with a shocking, serious suicide.

The melodramatics of the Berkeley production piece may seem to be divorced from the comedy. If, however, we see the overall tone of the musical as one of gaiety and freedom, some of the essential qualities of a spirit of play and laughter can be realised. The musical comedy obviously is a rambling, disjointed, dramatic form with its spirit bent more towards comedy even when the plot often seems serious. Using a plot that is centred on producing a play, *42nd Street*, like so many musicals, is essentially serious. Throughout the Thirties only a few musicals employed a comic leading character who could be labelled the protagonist. Guy Kibbee's portrait of the "dirty old man" who is chasing the star of the company functions as a supporting role rather than a main one. One minor character, played by Ned Sparks, offers an occasional dry, sarcastic bit of verbal wit. The pattern of the musical seems to have been moulded, and only occasionally did a comic lead become the focus of the plot. Seldom did a fully-fledged musical develop a strong comic plot line with many comic situations. Furthermore, this type of film often was burdened with song and dance entertainers who lacked comic and acting talent. Dick Powell, a feature player in so many musicals, had at best a sterile charm but never gave a spark of full-blooded manhood to his roles; he always seemed like the drugstore mannequin. Ruby Keeler, in *42nd Street* and other musicals, was painfully inadequate as an actress—she appeared to be reading her lines from a "idiot board." And, strange as it may seem, her singing was next to awful. Only her hoofing (early two-dimensional tap) was passable.

With their precursor of the age breaking box-office records, Warner Brothers produced *Gold Diggers of 1933,* a carbon copy of this previous effort. Directly from *42nd Street* came Ruby Keeler, Dick Powell, Ginger Rogers, Guy Kibbee, and Ned Sparks. Busby Berkeley once more handled the choreography. Two more comedians, Sterling Holloway and Tammany Young, fleshed out the comedy somewhat, but it was standard fair. Once more a young man (Dick Powell) was in love with a young woman (Ruby Keeler), but this time the man was a song writer and the plot involved the man's success rather than the rise of a chorus girl to stardom. Tuneful music, "We're in the Money," "Pettin' in the Park," and "Forgotten Men" helped to sell the musical to the public as did Berkeley's involved "shadow waltz" which incorporated a chorus of girls in tripledecked hoop skirts playing phosphorescent violins. When the lights went out, an overhead shot revealed the many violins forming a huge bull fiddle.

Cynically, Warners declared there would be no more musical features from its studios "until the imitative craze dies down," but by the end of the year the company had another hit and probably the best of this type of film. *Footlight Parade* had an asset that other works lacked—James Cagney. The actor had played a series of roles: a gambler, gangster, taxi-driver, and auto-racer. Fresh from the part of a sleazy entrepreneur of marathon dance and a scheme to promote a fake weight reducer in *Hard to Handle,* released early in 1933, Cagney had the breezy aggressiveness that pulled the picture together and made it move. Director Lloyd Bacon had profited from his direction of *42nd Street* and evidently had a strong hand in assisting Cagney. In *42nd Street* Warner Baxter's character of a Broadway director was stodgily serious about his theatrical enterprise—as if he were pulling together a Greek or Shakespearian tragedy. Young Cagney, in the role of a director, had the fire and style for the musical that Baxter lacked. He also proved himself a formidable song and dance man with skill in exchanging wisecracks with his cast and backers. A master at the "put down," he attacked a censor played by Hugh Herbert. In a dance routine featuring a chorus of mechanical dolls Herbert objected: "You must put banners on those dolls. You know . . . Connecticut." Rebuking him and confusing the geography of the New England states (thus, a double "put down" was achieved) he cracked: "What do they have to do in Massachusetts, wear red flannel drawers?"

Footlight Parade is replete with this kind of humour—the wisecrack and the "put down."

Granted, the picture does not have the wit of the sophisticated comedy of *Twentieth Century* (1934) with screenplay by Ben Hecht and Charles MacArthur (based on a stageplay by Charles Bruce Millhalland), but it has many characteristics that move in this direction. The dialogue is crisp and moves slickly in a way seldom witnessed in the musical of the Thirties. Screenwriters Mannel Seff and James Seymour didn't quite reach the level which a critic could call literate drama or a work of high. wit, but they provided a much stronger vehicle than was typical of the period. Cagney and his director Bacon made up the difference.

Not without its faults, the film used Ruby Keeler and Dick Powell. However, their talents were more confined to the song and dance division—fortunately, they were given less dialogue than in their previous musicals. Frank McHugh as the fussy dance director helped with his comedy of frustration and thereby muted some of the inadequacy of Miss Keeler and Powell in the rehearsal scenes.

As evident in most musicals of the period, the novelty and the garish spectacle caught the critics' as well as the public's eye. *Footlight Parade* was called the "most lavish of the screen musical works" by the *Literary Digest* of October 21, and the review in this publication noted that sequences were so elaborate they couldn't be done on the Broadway stage. Berkeley once more had three gaudy numbers, "Honeymoon Hotel," "By a Waterfall," and "Shanghi Lil." Humour in the first leaned toward the sly sexual nature (both illicit and legalised) of men and women in hotels. Tasteless by some people's standards was the presence of a little, precocious boy who engaged in peeking at "honeymooners" in various rooms of the hotel. In "By a Waterfall" much water and near nudity of women produced the most lavish water ballet ever filmed. Taking over for a drunken leading song and dance man, James Cagney executed the miracle of the man who performs the unlikely, ad lib, last minute, brilliant performance to save the show. In "Shanghi Lil" he tapped, marched, and sang with the vigour of a star; in his own brilliant and sometimes hammy way he even made Ruby Keeler a part of the show.

Most musicals of the Thirties existed in the strange, dramatic world of disunity. Somehow *Footlight Parade* had enough going for it to override the fault. The love life of the director had enough comic elements as did his struggle to produce a show. Most works seemed to have comedy grafted to a serious plot. Broader humour always was created by such comics as Guy Kibbee, Hugh Herbert, Frank McHugh, Victor Moore or Edward Everett Horton. Such character comedians were usually given supporting or even minor roles in musical films. Therefore, much of the comedy created by the leads (if it was created at all) was of a light, romantic quality that seldom promoted laughter beyond a chuckle.

A direction that might have produced more risible musicals was born when Eddie Cantor starred in the feature *Palmy Days* in 1931. While it is a mixed *genre* with a strong comedy plot line, the work has three production numbers and a total of four songs. The framework has a musical pattern. Pitted against a tall, horsy, blonde comedienne, Charlotte Greenwood, Cantor has a foil— a man chaser that brings out the best of his comic character. Eddie sings and dances in such numbers as "Nothing Too Good for My Baby" and "My Honey Said Yes, Yes." His 1932 *The Kid from Spain* opens with a big production number and uses a total of six musical elements in the picture. Comedy is achieved from his attempt to be a bullfighter, but, as in the 1931 work, the best comedy develops when he is the reluctant lover who is pursued by an aggressive woman. Blunt, *risqué* wit makes the picture a delight to see even today.

But Cantor hit his stride with the marvellous vehicle *Roman Scandals* the next year (1933). Even though about seven people, George S. Kaufman, Robert E. Sherwood, William Anthony McGuire, George Oppenheimer, Arthur Sheekman, Nat Perrin, and Cantor, had a hand in writing the script, the film has a unity and tightness that make it superior to most works of its kind. Costing over a million depression dollars, *Roman Scandals* was producer Samuel Goldwyn's bid to compete with the rash of musicals produced during that year.

Focusing on the fantasy of an eccentric grocer's errand boy (Cantor), the bulk of the plot develops in the form of a boy's dream that he is in ancient Rome. About to be sold as a slave at public auction, the young man discovers that few people will bid for him because he is so scrawny. Eddie gets into the act by becoming a pitchman for his own services as a slave: "I can cook a little. I can take care of the children. If there are no children, I can take care of that." He also proves he can entertain by doing a little dance and singing "All of me—why not take all of me." When a

rich, old hag starts bidding for him, he prefers a male sadist with a whip. The exchange with the elderly, ugly woman goes like this:

EDDIE: I'm weak. I can't do any work.
WOMAN: *(slyly)* I'm not buying you for work.
EDDIE: Just what I was afraid of.

Through a series of comic complications Eddie finally becomes a court jester for Emperor Valerius (Edward Arnold). Humour develops from anachronism when Eddie refers constantly to the Twentieth century world. Trying to tell jokes with such references, he leaves the court confused. Not understanding his allusion to Mickey and Minnie Mouse, Valerius asks if Minnie is also a mouse. "Sure. Otherwise it would be very inconvenient," Eddie explains.

Many facets of the comedian's skill develop in this picture. He exhibits comic cowardice, a con-man's ability to bilk authority, and a child-like spirit of play when faced with each new situation. Visually, Cantor becomes as adroit as he does verbally. Many of his reactions, the rolling of his large eyes, the gaiety of movement, the charming smile, and the overall warmth of a little fellow struggling against odds and escaping are intriguing. His aggression is distinctive, but he never becomes the brash con-man in the vein that later was to be developed by Phil Silvers.

Comic ingenuity abounds as the little fellow escapes one situation after another. When he hides in a harem, he finds it necessary to use a mud pack over his face, neck, and legs. Pretending to be a mysterious doctor from a foreign country who has arrived to assist the women of the harem, he breaks into a blackface routine from vaudeville. Eventually, this sequence becomes a big Berkeley production number, "Keep Young and Beautiful," a delightful song by Harry Warren and Al Dubin. All but one of the musical numbers (a serious torch song "No More Love") feature Cantor as soloist. As he takes the lead in the intricately staged numbers and the center of the whole plot, the total film becomes his. In the musical with a strong comedy emphasis, he can be rated as king of them all. By 1933 he was the highest paid comedian in the country; not merely through his films but also as America's leading radio comedian. In fact, his success in that medium cut into the number of films he created in the Thirties, and consequently, his influence on the musical began to wane.

In his 1932 autobiography, *My Life Is in Your Hands,* Cantor explained his success in moving to New York and into a radio contract:

Every Sunday night at eight o'clock I went on the air for Chase and Sanborn's coffee and Eddie Cantor's bread and butter. In the brief twenty-one weeks that I broadcast, I established the unique record of becoming the Number One attraction of the air, excelling in point of popularity the oldest and most established features on any program. It isn't nice for me to say this, but it's true. This proved easily to be the peak of my career thus far . . .

It is however, only conjecture that Cantor may have changed the face of the musical. *Roman Scandals* may have been a fortunate combination of writing, directing, and production talents that could not be equalled in a later picture. The disjointed variety show characteristics seeped into his next film. Appearing with Ethel Merman, Ann Sothern, and George Murphy in *Kid Millions* (1934), his talents were dampened in the first half by the "show biz on board a ship" type of plot and in the second half by a farcical conflict with a sultan and his daughter in a strange mid-Eastern country that was half Arabic and half Egyptian. It was two films badly grafted together and once more bearing the earmark of a musical. Even veteran comedy director Roy Del Ruth couldn't put together this script that had been concocted by Arthur Sheekman, Nat Perrin, and Nunnally Johnson. Romantic lead George Murphy proved to be even duller than Dick Powell although Ann Sothern as his girl was charming and winsome. In the last half of the film Eddie met the sultan's daughter (Jesse Block) and thereby had a comic foil without the talent of Charlotte Greenwood of *Palmy Days*. Obviously a comedienne from heavy handed vaudeville, Miss Block was unrestrained to the point of being silly and hammy. In *Kid Millions* Cantor once more created his best humour when he was faced with the daughter and the sultan ordered him boiled in oil: "Take the dog away!" he cried. Eddie questioned the sultan, "Her?" and the father replied, "No, you." Naturally, as much as Eddie's comic character revealed cowardice, he preferred death to the aggressive female. But (in a slapstick filled final sequence) Eddie escaped in an airplane that he could not fly.

Cantor's ability to turn a line, even a mediocre one, was an asset that made him a successful radio comedian, but he was skilled in visual comedy as well. It was a pity that he made so much money in radio that he did not concentrate on films. Even second-rate Cantor was better than most of the musical comedy works of the Thirties.

Two types of musical comedy had not fully developed by the end of 1933—the kind that starred a dancer and the kind that starred a singer. However, that year embryonic evidence of these types could be witnessed when Fred Astaire and Ginger Rogers, as supporting players, were teamed in *Flying Down to Rio,* and Bing Crosby appeared in *College Humor, Too Much Harmony,* and *Going Hollywood.* Essentially, Miss Rogers, Astaire, and Crosby were still only one part of the total variety-musical film and not the protagonists of the total movie drama. They would arrive in such leading positions as the decade progressed and reach the peak of their success in the Forties.

Flying Down to Rio was RKO's venture into the 1933 fad of musicals that led (in subsequent pictures) to the dance team of Miss Rogers and Astaire. Not the most humorous of the musical comedy species, the sub-*genre* that developed did feature the charm and freedom of the dance and, at times, a fully-fledged comic dance would be used in at least one number. A comic dance was not used in *Flying Down to Rio*. The exhilaration of Spanish music, however, was featured in "The Carioca." In an unlikely improvisation the couple "did their thing" in this number. The piece turned into an unimaginative production number which illustrated that Dave Gould as dance director had been influenced by Berkeley but had not yet developed the skills of the master. Toward the end of the film Fred Astaire indicated that he had already moved into more complicated dance routines by his creation of a rehearsal solo dance combining ballroom and ballet with the older tap routines.

As most musicals of this magic year tried to prove, the final piece in *Flying Down to Rio* is the "kicker" for the whole *soufflé*. Now only fascinating because it can be termed "ridiculous camp," the episode displays girls strapped in various poses onto the wings of airplanes. To the strains of an orchestra on the ground, the chorus girls do various, but obviously limited, routines as the planes fly over the hotel. All this is done to the tune of "Flying Down to Rio" and in the wildest of musical fantasies, no one doubts the physical feats—that the gals can do their routines on the planes and hear the orchestra on the ground above the roar of the airplane motors. Suspension of belief in ordinary limitations must be stronger in the audience that witnesses a musical.

Flying Down to Rio is, by modern critical standards, a routine musical of the period, but it did promote the career of Fred Astaire. He appeared in many works with Ginger Rogers and later had other dance partners: Rita Hayworth, Cyd Charisse, Jane Powell, Leslie Caron, and Judy Garland. He was even teamed with his rising competitor, Gene Kelly, in *Ziegfeld Follies* (1946) for the number "The Babbit and the Bromide." Astaire, of course, cannot be described as a comedian in the true sense; he was more of a breezy young man who later became a breezy, fantastically agile older man who could act successfully in light comedy works. Furthermore, he was able to execute effective comic dance routines such as his tramp dance with Judy Garland in *Easter Parade* (1948). His ten films in the Thirties established him as the leading dancer of the musical.

Bing Crosby might also be classified as a light comedian who used the charm of his own personality in much the same way that Astaire did. At the beginning of the Thirties Bing acted in two-reel comedies under Mack Sennett's direction. These frail, very thin little comedies had qualities similar to the feature musical. In *Bring on Bing* (circa 1931) the crooner received his acting lessons and sang two songs. He was very popular as a singer in films and on radio in the Thirties. He appeared in twenty-one features during the decade —most often in college pictures, "broadcast," and "follies" type creations which merely displayed him as the crooner—one of the "grand hotel" variety of talents. By 1936 in *Pennies from Heaven* he began to receive stronger parts and star billing. He was to achieve even greater success in the Second World War period of the Forties when he was teamed with Bop Hope in the famous "road pictures" of which *The Road to Singapore* (1940) was their first work.

The decline of the musical with its standard show business formula was obvious in *Gold Diggers of 1935*. With the total drama under Busby Berkeley's direction, the feeble plot limped along with a story of a rich woman's use of the variety show for her favourite charity. By this time the self-imposed censorship of the movie industry had left the musical without its former bluntness and earthiness. The comic efforts of Hugh Herbert and Frank McHugh and the muggings of Adolphe Menjou as an egocentric, con-artist stage director did not get the drama off the ground. Dick Powell

was as bland as ever, and his tenor musical renditions as expressionless as they had been from the beginning of his career. Only the spectacular "Lullaby of Broadway" number at the end of the film indicated that Berkeley still had retained some of his magic.

The popularity of the musical and the variety show waxed and waned with each year during the Thirties. How the variety show still persisted might be questioned by some today. All one need do is look at television to find the answer. Today, as in the Thirties, this form of light, desultory entertainment passes the time and sometimes can be most enjoyable if one doesn't mind being bored while he waits for an act or a turn that fits his taste. In 1938 *The Goldwyn Follies* employed all the types of entertainment that graced the vaudeville stage at the turn of the century. Radio favourites Kenny Baker, Phil Baker, and Edgar Bergen and Charlie McCarthy were used in the production. Ballerina Vera Zorina and operatic star Helen Jepson also appeared. Comedy was provided by the Ritz Brothers and Bobby Clark. Odd as it may seem, this whole concoction was scripted by Ben Hecht, a writer who had some good works to his credit. The piece is viewed today merely as a period curiosity which reflects the feebleness of most of the "follies" and "broadcast" films of the period.

The last half of the Thirties also marked the invasion of the child stars. With the presence of moppets and teenagers came even simpler and less comic sentimental musicals. Although not confined to the younger set, the sentimental musical, the antithesis of the "bawdy, gaudy" works of 1933, began its reign. Shirley Temple, one of the first moppets to catch the eye and the heart of the public, entered show business with simple song and dance routines. Her features leaned toward the musical, but most of her works were sentimental comedies with musical segments. Such works were *The Little Colonel* (1935), *Captain January* (1936) and *Heidi* (1937). Her 1938 *Little Miss Broadway* best fit the pattern of the musical. Seven musical numbers, with one repeated among them, illustrated the pattern, with a final elaborate production piece using the title song. George Murphy becomes her adult dancing partner in this work, and it may have been a clever bit of casting because his skills in this department are so limited that the darling of America was never upstaged. It is interesting to note that her popularity was so great at this time she was the leading figure in *Little Miss Broadway.* She becomes a little Miss Fixit for all the adults around her, and she is the featured singer in all the musical numbers. The comedy created by her character taking action in the world of adults is very light—the chuckle variety, and the total film has story elements replete with sentiment. While the play on the emotions becomes quite sticky for a modern day audience, it must be admitted that there is a warmth and a charm in the movie that has appeal—a spirit of sentimental comedy that no longer exists today.

One of the most moronic musicals to be created in the cinema of the period was the Busby Berkeley directed *Babes in Arms* (1939). Two talents, Judy Garland and Micky Rooney, that were soon to appear in better works, are shown engaged in creating a musical to prove to their show biz parents that they are not "babes in arms." There is a marching song of the kids created by Rodgers and Hart which has the unbelievably bad Hart lyrics, "They call us babes in arms, but we're babes in armour . . ." sung by an operatic baritone "kid" who must have reached puberty much earlier than the rest of those in the cast. This grand march with the title song occurs in the first half of the film. Unfortunately, the work degenerates even further. Humour is so pointless that the writers try to develop chuckles from Mickey Rooney's superficial attempt to be a big deal director. Reaching for maturity he smokes a cigar and gets sick. Also, light comedy is achieved by a triangle romance among the characters played by Judy Garland, Mickey Rooney, and June Preisser. Mickey achieves some light humour as a director who imitates, with a fair amount of talent, the famous actors Clark Gable and Lionel Barrymore in order to tell two of his actors how to do a scene. However, the whole film is so inane that when it is viewed today one suspects the taste of those who liked the work when it was first shown. It might make today's generation believe that their parents were fools to live in an age that produced such drivel. Only one bright moment seems to remain in the picture. There is a brilliant, yes, even sentimental, moment when Judy Garland expresses in song a teenage love for her idol, Clark Gable. Her rendition of "I Cried for You" is almost worth the struggle of viewing the whole picture.

What might be described as the operetta, a musical type that became popular in this decade, need not be explored in detail since it contained few memorable comic scenes. Appealing to the romantic and sentimental temperament of the times, it often featured the heroic leading man played woodenly by Nelson Eddy and sweet leading woman enacted with laboured coyness by Jeanette MacDonald. Typical of the genre is *Rose Marie* (1936), a musical focusing on the fortunes of a Canadian mounted policeman and his sweetheart in a romanticised, Hollywood "Northwest" setting. Even though the taste for screen operetta was on the wane by 1940, it did influence the use of this kind of music in some sentimental comedies. Teenage sopranos, Deanna Durbin* and, in the Forties, Gloria Jean, cashed in on the taste for light opera in small doses.

From the sentimental musical came one masterpiece that has the charm, cleverness, colour, and universality today that it possessed in 1939. *The Wizard of Oz* may be considered not only one of the best musical comedies of the Thirties, but one of the best of all times. Critics probably have ignored the worth of this film because they consider it "kid stuff" and consequently not on a level for serious consideration. Authors who have written books focusing on their choice of fifty best films, Bosley Crowther and David Zinman, do not place it among the top titles, although Crowther does give it some rank by placing it on his "supplemental list of one hundred distinguished films." With his list is one "kid stuff" film, *Pinocchio,* and musicals such as *Meet Me in St. Louis* (1944), *Singin' in the Rain* (1952), and *Top Hat* (1935). Critics have seldom smiled favourably at musicals or at films that seem directed to an audience of children. Even the industry's Academy Awards had some difficulty recognising *The Wizard of Oz* in 1939, but it should be realised that the film was pitted against such movies as *Gone with the Wind* (the winner), *Goodbye Mr. Chips, Mr. Smith Goes to Washington, Stagecoach,* and *Wuthering Heights.* Since special awards in the musical phase of production were available to *The Wizard of Oz,* Herbert Stothart won an Oscar for the best original musical score and Harold Arlen won one for his song "Over the Rainbow." *Gone with the Wind,* of course, won most of the awards, and the director of that work, Victor Fleming, also directed *The Wizard of Oz.*

The value of this children's classic, adapted

---

*Chapter Eight explores the characteristics of Miss Durbin's *That Certain Age* (1938).

from the book by L. Frank Baum, as a musical of the Thirties becomes clearer when it is thoroughly examined and related to other films of the *genre*. *The Wizard of Oz* is strong in all phases of its creation. The tight dramatic plot line and basic comic complications were deftly handled by writers Noel Langley, Florence Ryerson, and Edgar Allen Wolfe. Director Fleming, who has distinguished himself as a director of such children's classics as *Treasure Island* (1935) and *Captains Courageous* (1938), maintained a firm grip on his material. Five comic characters in the cinema drama proved to be an integral part of the total drama, and the actors playing the roles were brilliant in their portrayals. Frank Morgan as Professor Marvel and the Wizard displayed all his comic skills by enacting a gate keeper, a cockney cab driver, and a guard—all three separate characters enacted by Professor Marvel to safeguard his feigned role as Wizard. Bert Lahr, seldom used effectively as a film comedian, created with warmth and vigour the most memorable role of his career, that of Cowardly Lion. Also completely absorbed in his role was Ray Bolger as Scarecrow. While not given as flashy a role, Jack Haley produced a subtle comic portrait of Tin Woodman. To this foursome add the comic villain, Witch, played by Margaret Hamilton, and you have a group of characters in a story enacted by excellent character actors with a finesse that would appeal to all ages for all times.

Judy Garland's contribution as Dorothy cannot be overlooked. Under Fleming's direction she handled the role effectively. With a character of limited range, she exuded warmth and charm. She seemed stilted only in the framework of the story, the scenes in the real world of Kansas. In the fairy land over the rainbow the seventeen-year-old actress seemed both sincere and believable. Her imagination worked best in the make-believe universe, but some of the sentiment of the Kansas scenes was too thick and sticky for an inexperienced actress to handle. However, her delivery of the curtain line, "Oh, Aunt Em, there's no place like home!" for example, might be considered difficult for even a seasoned actress.

Obviously, a musical could not exist without effective lyrics and tunes. E. Y. Harburg and Harold Arlen had the hit of their careers. Almost every song, twelve in all, had clever lyrics and catchy tunes. Not only were such songs as "Over the Rainbow," "Merry Old Land of Oz," "Ding Dong, the Witch Is Dead," and "If I Only Had a Brain," immediate successes, they are songs that do not grow old.

One feature of *The Wizard of Oz* that made it a precursor of the whole movement of the Forties musicals was the effective integration of songs and production numbers into the total drama. Choreographer Bobby Connolly and director Fleming obtained unity by fusing these phases of the production in a way that had not been fully achieved in the musical of the Thirties.

As a musical with an emphasis on comedy, *The Wizard of Oz* had many songs with humorous lyrics. "If I Only Had a Brain" was first sung by Ray Bolger and repeated with the substitution of the desires of Tin Woodman for a heart and Cowardly Lion for courage. Very clever lyrics also are in the song delivered by Bert Lahr—"If I Were King." Employing extensive vibrato, the comedian used a parody of an operatic baritone when he declared, "If I were king of the forest, not queen, not duke, not prince . . ." He continued by pointing out that he would be dressed in satin, and mountains would bow; bulls would "cow-cow"; rabbits would respect him, and chipmunks would genuflect in his presence.

Lahr's timing of the spoken dialogue also proved an asset when, as Cowardly Lion, he suddenly burst forth bravely in an attempt to rescue Dorothy from the castle of the witch:

COWARDLY LION: I'll tear 'em apart! Woof! I may not come out alive, but I'm going in there. There's only one thing I want you fellows to do.
TIN WOODMAN AND SCARECROW: What's that?
COWARDLY LION: *(pathetically)* Talk me out of it.

Clever humour developed during the revelation scene when the wizard was exposed as a fake who was really Professor Marvel:

SCARECROW: You're a humbug!
PROFESSOR MARVEL: *(meekly)* Yes. Yes. Exactly so. I'm a humbug.
DOROTHY: You're a very bad man.
PROFESSOR MARVEL: No, my dear, I'm a very good man. I'm just a very bad wizard.

The "professor" proceeded to award prizes to those he had promised to help. To Scarecrow he indicated that the brain was a "very mediocre commodity" possessed by even crawling creatures. "Back where I come from," he continued, "we have universities, seats of great learning, where men go to become great thinkers. And when they come out, they think deep thoughts and with no more brains than you have. But, they have one thing you haven't got—a diploma." He then awarded Scarecrow a degree of Th.D.—Doctor of Thinkology. Cowardly Lion was reminded that war heroes "once a year take their fortitude out of moth balls and parade it down the main street of the city," and was given a medal for bravery. Then Professor Marvel told Tin Woodman that what he needed was given to "good deed doers" and proceeded to deliver the *cliché* banquet recognition: "Therefore, in consideration of your kindness, I take pleasure at this time in presenting you with a small token of our esteem and affection." Thus, society's scholars, heroes, and philanthropists were deftly satirised by actor Frank Morgan in the resolution of the adventures in the land of Oz.

Some of the best characteristics of the Thirties musical can be summed up by looking at *The Wizard of Oz*'s virtues. There is gaiety, warmth, and an unpretentious spirit of play in the best

works of this kind. Character actors at the peak of their activity in this period contributed greatly to the comedy of the film. While many of the later works, in the Forties and Fifties, were self-consciously clever and cute, there seemed to be a flair in that age, almost a naïveté according to some, that gave these films a freshness which has never been captured since.

On the other hand, there are critics of the musical who prefer the productions of the Forties and Fifties. Douglas McVay in *The Musical Film* and John Springer in *All Talking! All Singing! All Dancing!* hold this view. There are two schools of thought, and I guess I must straddle the fence; there are different qualities to be appreciated in the musicals of these various periods. For me, most aspects of the musical's production in the Forties and Fifties improved. The story and acting in the best works improved, but comedy in the films made little progress and generally faded.

In *42nd Street* (1933) Warner Baxter (center) proves to be a slave-driving director for a Broadway musical production.

A posed shot for *Footlight Parade* (1933) showing
Ruby Keeler, James Cagney, Joan Blondell, Frank
McHugh and Dick Powell.

Producer Cagney shows dance director Frank McHugh
the proper step for a routine in *Footlight Parade*.

A *Palmy Days* (1931) publicity still with Charlotte Greenwood and Eddie Cantor.

Ironically turning his attention more to radio, Eddie Cantor was one of the few comedians given leading roles in musicals.

Cantor does a dance for a palace guard. A posed shot for *Roman Scandals* (1933).

Ginger Rogers and Fred Astaire in supporting roles for *Flying Down to Rio* (1933).

The reunion of Ginger and Fred in *Barkleys of Broadway* (1949).

Top Hat (1935) with Miss Rogers and Astaire.

In *Pennies from Heaven* (1938), Edith Fellows, Donald Meek, and Bing Crosby.

Dick Powell and Gloria Stuart provide the romantic interest in *Gold Diggers of 1935*.

Over fifty girls and fifty pianos for "The Words Are in My Heart" production number, *Gold Diggers of 1935*.

Gold Diggers of 1935 used this high angle shot for the "Lullaby of Broadway" production number.

Shirley Temple dances for the courtroom in *Little Miss Broadway* (1938).

In *Little Miss Broadway* George Murphy assists Miss Temple.

The more genteel, "high-brow" operetta, *Rose Marie* (1936), starring Jeanette MacDonald and Nelson Eddy.

Scarecrow (Ray Bolger) and Dorothy (Judy Garland)
help the rusty Tin Woodman (Jack Haley) to walk
in the 1939 *The Wizard of Oz.*

The quartet of adventurers take a ride in *The Wizard
of Oz* as Frank Morgan plays a cockney cab driver
as well as Wizard.

Dorothy comforts Cowardly Lion (Bert Lahr) in *The Wizard of Oz.*

4
Zanies in a Stage-Movieland

The phone rings at the hotel desk, and Groucho, as Mr. Hammer and manager of the establishment, answers it.

GROUCHO: Hello. Yes? Ice water in 318. Is that so? Where'd you get it? Oh, you want some? Oh, that's different. Have you got any ice? No, I haven't. This is Cocoanut Beach. No snow, no ice. Get some onions. That will make your eyes water. *(pause)* What? *(pause)* You too!

This outrageous pun (from the 1929 *Cocoanuts*) employs a play on words, using "ice" and "eyes," is an example of a staple for a Marx Brothers' movie. If you have an aversion to such humour, the manic team is not your meat. Both Groucho and Chico have many punch lines that depend on the pun. Although no one has bothered to count the times the two brothers use this comic device, it is safe to say that Chico uses it more often as his main technique for eliciting laughter. With an Italian dialect and a slow working brain, Chico not only speaks differently; it is obvious that he hears differently than anyone else. When Groucho explains a sanity clause at the end of a contract in *A Night at the Opera* (1935) Chico laughs and tries to prove he is a clever bargainer: "You can't fool me. There ain't no Sanatie Claus."

In Groucho's telephone monologue quoted above there were several elements of wit besides the pun. Character entered into the creation of comedy and an inversion of roles obviously was employed. Instead of displaying the fussy, obsequious air of a Franklin Pangborn type of hotel manager, Groucho took pleasure in cutting all his guests down to size. In each of his movies his character had the basic facet of the "put down" or "cut down" artist whose life flourishes best when he verbally assaults everyone—especially those with pretensions or an air of superiority. In her many roles as the bovine dowager, Margaret Dumont became the butt of his invective. He constantly took swipes at her size, face, age, and intellect. In his relationship with her it became obvious that he was totally anti-romantic. When she was an object of matrimony, it was merely to get at her money.

Closely tied to this character facet in the above telephone monologue was Groucho's constant chatter. The con-man in him emerged when asked a question, and he sometimes artfully and sometimes awkwardly talked the issue to death. He often ventured onto weird tangents, in a stream of conscious establishment of his wacky ideas on just about everything and anything. A word or phrase often sparked a chain reaction of delightful pseudo-logic that almost sounded valid. More than any other comedian of the Thirties, he revelled in this device. Of his many *non sequiturs,* there were some clever, quotable gags that won him a high reputation. He is reported to have made a comment something like this: "I wouldn't belong to an organisation that would have me as a member." More specifically, in *A Day at the Races* (1937), he, as a quack doctor taking the pulse of Harpo, delivered another classic one-liner: "Either this man is dead or my watch has stopped." Such mind joggling bits of humour caught the attention of all lovers of word play and wacky logic. The Marx Brothers became the darlings of some of the leading humorous writers in the states. Alex Woollcott, Robert Benchley, Franklin P. Adams, George S. Kaufman, and Dorothy Parker loved their work and became their personal friends.

But the wit of the Marx Brothers was not merely

verbal. Their visual gags and reactions were enhanced by the camera. Harpo, as a mute comedian, naturally profited from the medium's ability to catch and emphasise all the details of his mime. Reactions to situations, as well as dialogue between Groucho and Chico, also were given added punch. Chases which had been employed on the stage and the often used musical chairs boudoir scenes that demanded many exits and entrances of the trio became more effective when developed in the movies. Later, when the climax of their pictures related more directly to the chase and fight conclusions of the silent film comedy, their films were definitely helped by the assets of the medium. In the 1935 *A Night at the Opera*'s climactic sequence, a chase during the performance of *Il Trovatore* provided the culmination of the total picture. The war game carried out by the four brothers in *Duck Soup* (1933) developed into an orgy of rapid fire visual and verbal gags which became the apex of the work. Without the use of the full powers of the medium, these two films, rated as the best of the Marx Brothers, would be flat and would lack the development and drive to be successful pictures.

More than those of any other major comedians of the Thirties, the Marx Brothers' films were tied to the musical comedy. Every one of their works retained songs, dances, instrumental solos by Chico and Harpo (except *Duck Soup*), and musical elements that displayed the heritage of the variety show and musical comedy of the Twenties stage. The variety of entertainment that this tradition provided was greatly appreciated by the audiences of the period, but it gave many of their films an overall desultory quality that would prevent them from standing the test of time. The relatively simple vaudeville skills of Chico on the piano and Harpo on the harp are now merely curiosities for modern day audiences. Aesthetically, interludes of this nature now become an intrusion on the plot, and a viewer today is sometimes inclined to agree on a serious level with Groucho's humorous put-down of Chico as he approached a piano in *Horse Feathers* (1932). Groucho looked directly at the camera, and consequently at the audience, as he declared: "I've got to stay here, but there's no reason why you folks shouldn't go out into the lobby until this thing blows over." This theatrical aside was treading on ground which revealed some of the basic vaudeville ramblings of the brothers, but the virtues, fortunately, outweighed the vices.

Their first film, *Cocoanuts* (1929), produced in the Paramount Astoria studio on Long Island, reflected all the characteristics of the Broadway musical transferred to the film medium in the formative period of sound movies. In the accepted fashion of the Twenties and early Thirties, it was burdened with a sub-plot centring on romantic leads, so that portions of the film now look slow, dull, and artless. But there were more problems than the taste of the times. The performances of the two leads were weak even for the critics of 1929. The acting and singing of Mary Eaton and Oscar Shaw almost condemned the piece to a state of an odd historical item that mirrored the defects and, at times, the charm of the Twenties musical. But, the Marx Brothers, despite the heavy anchor, had some good moments that got their vehicle sailing from the harbour, although not to the destination that would make the venture a success. *Cocoanuts* was more than a weak recording of a stage musical; it was a prelude of things to come—when the team, under effective direction, would produce their particular vaudeville-movie comedies with all their best talents effectively integrated into the total work.

An examination of all the Marxes' movies reveals that the major portions of their films are stage oriented. They often face the camera and do a routine; many actions occur using a standard long shot with a few close cut-ins to show reactions of the characters involved. Only in their chase and fight scenes do their films take on a cinematic dimension that divorces the work from its vaudeville heritage. While some evaluators may find this limited use of the medium a defect, I believe that the content of a scene, the skill of the performers, and the material being used, can transcend all the limitations of the cinema. Chaplin's films have been termed "stagy," but even when the camera functions as a recorder of his performance, the results are brilliant. Most directors of the Marx Brothers realised when the actor and his routine were to take over—the camera then served as an observer-recorder of a stage play.

Cocoanuts displays the overall design of a musical. Containing eight musical elements spaced throughout the show, it has three production numbers (some combined with vocals), piano, harp, and clarinet instrumentals by Chico and Harpo, a dance number, and solos by the romantic leads. Such a pattern, with variations, would provide the basis for future Marx Brothers' productions. Even with this much music, there is an emphasis on the comedy created by Groucho, Chico, and Harpo. Zeppo plays a minor, straight part and, only occasionally, as in his role for *Horse Feathers* (1932), does he play a prominent part in their comedies.

A Groucho monologue to his hotel staff at the beginning of *Cocoanuts* indicates the nature of his contribution to the brothers' movies in the Thirties. First of all, his monologues show him as the ringmaster of the whole three-ring circus. The antics of Chico and Harpo may send the drama on tangents, but it eventually returns to Groucho and his problems, the centre of the plot. In this particular film we see his con-man's distorted logic (a basis of his character in most films) when he convinces a gullible staff that they should not be "wage slaves" by requesting their salary. He wants them not to be tied to conventional attitudes:

> I want you to be free! Remember, there's nothing like liberty—except *Collier's* and the *Saturday Evening Post*. Be free, my friends. One for all and all for me, and me for you and three for five, and six for a quarter.

Such wacky monologues would be used again and again in the films. In this case a burlesque of the nonsense a leader spouts to the crowd comes close to satire. But the assault on logic does not end here. It continues as the leader tries to give a sop to his audience. When he receives a telegram that looks as if the hotel might get some business, he comes to an odd postscript. It reads: "Aunt Fanny had an eight pound boy. Can you come to the wedding?" To his staff he assures, "You see, everything is all right, boys. Everything is all right. You're all invited to the wedding of Aunt Fanny's eight pound boy." This type of far-out humour was Groucho's stock in trade.

Groucho also proves to be forever "on the make" when he deals with individuals. Delivering a spiel to Margaret Dumont who plays the role of Mrs. Potter, he describes the glories and intricacies of Florida real estate with the same mosaic and jumble of ideas and phrases that characterised his speech to his hotel staff. More effective wit develops later, however, when Groucho employs insults in a courtship scene. A gold mine of invective comedy evolves when Miss Dumont becomes the object of his financial desires. A rich widow with money bag shape, Mrs. Potter gets blasted fully:

MR. HAMMER: Did anyone tell you, you looked like the Prince of Wales. I don't mean the present prince of Wales—one of the old wales. And believe me when I mean whales I mean whales. I know a whale when I see one. Did you say your room was 318? You know, I'm the proprietor of this hotel and I have a passkey to every room in it.
MRS. POTTER: Passkey?
MR. HAMMER: "Passkey." That's Russian for "pass" . . . (*He is, of course, making a pass at her. He rolls his eyes.*) Won't you lie down?

This kind of sexual attitude in Groucho's character was basic to its total make-up; evaluators recognise it but do not seem to see it as an important factor in all the comedian's comic portraits. It was a facet of the brothers' movies even after the strict 1934 Production Code of Ethics demanded the elimination of "obscenity in word, gesture, reference, song or by suggestion." More than any other comedians, Groucho and Harpo would be relatively untouched by the pronouncement of the Hay's Office. Groucho used the *double entendre* and the leer as he pursued the woman (Margaret Dumont or Thelma Todd) to the couch. Harpo employed the periodic pursuit of a woman who just passes by as a running gag in most of the pictures. But, it must be noted, such gags and the situations that motivated them were lighter in treatment in the later films and did not have the bite of the early Thirties works.

Groucho's "romantic" attack on Miss Dumont in *Cocoanuts* also displays the ludicrous simile: "Your eyes, your eyes, they shine like the pants of a blue serge suit." Furthermore, the union of Mrs. Potter and Mr. Hammer, according to Groucho's version of the easy life, would feature the woman coming down the path from work, with the man waiting at the gate. When his motives are suspect ("I don't think you'd love me if I were poor"), Groucho brashly replies with another example of his crafty, odd-ball logic, "I might, but I'd keep my mouth shut." When Groucho takes physical action, Miss Dumont rebukes him vehemently by telling him to keep his hands to himself. He strikes a wrestling pose and challenges her: "Come on, I'll play you one more game. Come on, the three of yah!"

The whole scene is a delightful burlesque of the marriage proposal and the sexual proposition. One of the longest scenes of this kind in a picture by the comedy team, it is also one of the best of its type executed by Groucho.

The visual humour in the Marx Brothers' films increased as their films moved from adaptations to scripts designed for the screen. Nevertheless, a great deal of visual comedy was already present in the stage production of *Cocoanuts*. Harpo can be credited with the lion's share of this type of humour. He had developed his mime in his vaudeville days.

According to his autobiography, *Harpo Speaks!*, the comedian decided to do what was called the dumb act, a category that also included jugglers, acrobats, and any pantomimists who did not use dialogue, when he took his Uncle Al's suggestion that such an act would bring more laughs for the team and when he realised that he couldn't out talk Groucho and Chico. As a full-time pantomimist, he equipped himself with an old bulb-type taxi-cab horn and a loud, frantic whistle (produced by his own lips) to assist in communication.

Harpo's most elaborate pantomime bit in *Cocoanuts* was executed when he displayed his wacky eating habits that seemed to be a counterpoint to Groucho's bizarre stream of conversation. For an appetiser he ate a sponge on the hotel main desk and drank the ink as if it were wine. Later in the film he consumed the mouth piece of an upright telephone.

Without the child-like attitudes and desires of Harpo's character such actions would merely seem silly—not something that could produce laughter. As the man-child engaged in a favourite game, he goes about his task of gobbling up each item as if it were food. To appreciate the comedian who developed such a character (silent screen comedian Harry Langdon had a similar portrait, and Stan Laurel's character was a case of arrested development), we must see the child-man in the role. More than any major comedian, Harpo employs for comic effect the nature of a child. Not only do inedible objects become food, but food becomes a cosmetic in *Night at the Opera* (1935). With a pancake as a powder puff he applies sugar, and with his finger he applies ketchup to his lips. The child-man plays the game of being a woman. But Harpo does not play the faggot—he has reached puberty. Well, he at least plays the game of reaching that stage of development. As a running gag in many of the films, he bolts from any of his strange endeavours, with a wild leer of a sex maniac, in pursuit of a passing female. According to Harpo this gag developed during the tour of *Cocoanuts*. He developed it as a visual ad lib to supplement one of Groucho's "quieter scenes." It was all part of the friendly, brotherly competition for laughs.

In this first film of the team Harpo used almost all his bag of tricks or, at least, the fundamental or formative shapes of them, as they would appear with slight variations in later films. Upon request or when a thing was merely mentioned in casual conversation, he pulled the most unlikely objects from the bottomless pockets of his shabby, oversized trench coat. Another gag was the offer of his leg instead of his hand when he first met someone. When the plot became dull, it sometimes seems, Harpo would throw a child-like fit of destructiveness. Anything that could be torn, detached, knocked off or stamped to a pulp received his full-fledged assault. In *Cocoanuts* he seemed more destructive than in any of his other films, but the malice of the screwy little eight-year-old down the block remained in his character throughout his career. In life, everyone reported, Adolph "Harpo" Marx was a mild-mannered, soft-spoken man.

Chico often functioned as a comrade and spokesman of Harpo or a feeder for Groucho's gags, but in *Cocoanuts* he did have a long scene that has always scored a hit when the picture has been shown. Allen Eyles in his *The Marx Brothers: Their World of Comedy* (A. Zwemmer and A. S. Barnes, 1966, pp. 26-27) quotes this "vy-a-duck" scene almost in total, so it need not be repeated here. In this scene Chico upsets Groucho who is giving him instructions. Groucho tells him of a viaduct leading over the mainland. Chico asks him, "Why a duck? Why-a no chicken?" An elaborate misalliance develops, with a complete lack of a "meeting of minds." A series of puns, misinterpretations, and arguments comes from Chico. Unlike Groucho's, Chico's handling of the English language is usually unconscious and consequently more laughable. When we see the exasperation and the put-down of the man (Groucho) who ordinarily engages in the activity for sport, we see some of the most hilarious comedy of a Marx Brothers' movie.

By filming one more of their stage successes, *Animal Crackers,* in 1930, the team added another picture to their credit. Although the work did not improve in handling the skills of the cinema medium, Groucho did shine in his fascinating portrayal of Captain Jeffrey T. Spaulding. In his introduction to the guests of the mansion, Captain Spaulding performs a delightful comic dance and song, displaying another talent that would become a Groucho trademark and would be incorporated in other pictures. He also used a more biting phase of his con-man character with the willing-to-be-bilked dowager, Mrs. Rittenhouse, played by Margaret Dumont. All the kindness of this rich woman was countered by blatant insults and an open display of greed; whenever the opportunity presented itself, Captain Spaulding turned on his heels to chase more desirable young women.

Groucho once more engages in his Lewis Carroll word games in *Animal Crackers* with the assistance of George S. Kaufman and Morris Ryskind—although it has been reported that the authors felt the Marx Brothers played havoc with their script. The whole film seems overly long and has only a few brilliant scenes to give it distinction.

In 1931, using the first original screenplay, the golden age of the Marx Brothers' movies began. During this period of seven years they produced five of their best features: *Monkey Business* (1931), *Horse Feathers* (1932), *Duck Soup* (1933), *Night at the Opera* (1935), and *Day at the Races* (1937). Present day critics and fans generally rate the last three as "top drawer" Marx Brothers, but it may be partly a result of these works receiving more showing than the others.

Monkey Business and *Horse Feathers* are two strong comedies that rank as high if not higher than any films of the *genre* produced in the early Thirties. With more viewings by those who appreciate this type of comedy, a wider, positive response for the works might be realised. Granted, serious flaws in story telling and some dull routines now net these two pictures mixed reactions. But there are overall controlling qualities of these films that make them a purer form of Marx Brothers' comedy. The romantic leads fade into the background as the brothers take over the total work. Except for the inevitable, diversive instrumentals by Chico and Harpo, the musical elements in the two movies seem to intrude less on the plot. The dash and gaiety of the team's performance, above all, give *Monkey Business* and *Horse Feathers* the comic brilliance that places the Marx Brothers among the kings of Thirties film comedy. All elements would be perfected in their 1933 work, *Duck Soup*.

Specific humorous highlights in *Monkey Business* can be revealed once more in the talents of Groucho. His Captain Spaulding of *Animal Crackers* was a step forward in relation to Mr. Hammer of *Cocoanuts*, but Groucho got bogged down in too much talk (as clever as some of it was) in both these stage adaptations. In *Monkey Business* Groucho's portrait of a con-man never borders on overexposure with too much verbiage; he has more drive and flair in his efforts to bed Mrs. Briggs, played by attractive Thelma Todd. Even his dia-

logue has more zip as he gives his comic *reductio ad absurdum* reason for being in a woman's bedroom closet:

MRS. BRIGGS: You can't stay in that closet.
GROUCHO: Oh, I can't, can I? That's what they said to Thomas Edison, mighty inventor; Thomas Lindberg, mighty flyer; and Tomashevsky, mighty like a rose. Just remember, my little cabbage, that if there weren't any closets, there wouldn't be any hooks, and if there weren't any hooks, there wouldn't be any fish, and that would suit me fine.

Later in the film he shows his fire as he makes more advances: "Mrs. Briggs, I've known and respected your husband Alky for many years, and what's good enough for him is good enough for me." He jumps on her lap.

Groucho even employs a homosexual gag when Alky, a tough gangster, admires his brashness:

ALKY BRIGGS: I could use a guy with your nerve. I think we could get along well together.
GROUCHO: *(coyly, rolling his eyes)* Well, of course, you see, we might have our little squabbles, but that's inevitable, don't you think?

All three of the Marx Brothers, Groucho, Chico, and Harpo, have more dash in *Monkey Business* when they become engaged in chase scenes. Action develops with a hide and seek game on board the ship when the four stowaways (Zeppo is still with the team) are chased by the captain and his crew. Harpo hides inside the stage of a puppet show while a performance is being given to children. Allen Eyles views this situation as developing into one of Harpo's most unique gags. From his hiding place the mute comedian starts getting into the act. With his famous "Gookie" expression, exaggerated, puffed up cheeks, and a pursed mouth, he becomes a puppet as his head pops into the proscenium arch of the little theatre. A poetic touch is added as the scene recalls the primitive origins of the brothers' madcap comedy—visions of travelling players of medieval times who performed shows at fairs and the later development of the strolling players, the *commedia dell' arte*, come to the mind of the critic.

While the 1932 *Horse Feathers* has many of the routine, derivative features of the college comedy pictures that date back to Harold Lloyd's *The Freshman* (1925), it also has the zest of comedy that moves, due to the efforts of the dedicated, forceful zanies with roots in the whole history of the humorous drama. Groucho, as a professor (a favourite in vaudeville skits) and head of Huxley college, adds another character to his repertoire. The standard play on words springs forth when an indignant father sees his son (Zeppo) with a girl on his lap: "Young lady, would you get up so I can see the son rise." He also tops this pun with a scolding of the boy by observing, "Doing your homework at school?" But the father is like the son and later displays an inversion of values gag as he pursues the son's girl. In the mock tones of a moralist Groucho discovers his son hiding in the girl's room while he is making amorous advances:

PROFESSOR WAGSTAFF: The shame of it, to see a son of mine trying to take a dame away from his father.
FRANK: Dad, I . . .
PROFESSOR WAGSTAFF: Enough of it. You leave immediately, and I'll stay and settle with this woman. And as soon as we're settled, we'll have you over for dinner.

Thus, the lechery of Groucho's character shines in *Horse Feathers* as it did in *Monkey Business* but with a hypocrisy that shows the vice in sharper comic tones. Also, a more vicious Groucho emerges with the assistance of the famous writer, S. J. Perelman, as Professor Wagstaff courts the girl (Thelma Todd) in a canoe. She tries to obtain the football signals of the Huxley team, and when he resists, uses baby talk: "Icky baby going to cwy." In a high register of his voice he savagely declares, "If icky girl keep talking that way big twong man goin' to kick all her teeth right down her throat."

With such an edge the usually mild football and college days picture takes on a new dimension that can be appreciated in our age of emphasis on anti-sentimental humour. With all its faults— a standard climactic winning of the game by unorthodox means plus uninspired Chico and Harpo routines—*Horse Feathers* holds up more effectively than most comedies of the period.

While anyone who prefers the Marx Brothers' *Duck Soup* (1933) to their *Night at the Opera* (1935) risks being dismissed as a structuralist or one who likes ordered, logical comedies by those critics who hold the view that a Marx comedy defies logic and order, I accept the label. To me *Duck Soup* is their best work. *Per se*, a well-structured comedy such as this does not hamper the quartet's effectiveness. *Horse Feathers* has a clear-cut and generally effective design, but it lacks the internal or organic unity that operates so effectively in *Duck Soup*. Chico and Harpo no longer seem to be only a part of the sub-plot that occasionally brushes into Groucho's world,

the main plot. In *Duck Soup* their routines fit the total pattern although they do have an elaborate, tangential routine with Edgar Kennedy. Their clever vaudeville turns eventually chalk up a unified whole. The climactic sequence is unique in their cinema. While the culminating episodes of *Monkey Business* and *Horse Feathers* made use of screen rather than stage techniques by employing an elaborate comic fight and a football game, such material had already been more skilfully handled in silent screen comedies. *Duck Soup*'s final war sequence seems tied to both the silent screen tradition and the sound film drama. A mosaic of wacky sights and sounds, this portion of the film is one of the best examples of what some critics call surrealism in the Marx Brothers. No other comedy has captured this strange wild world of war with such weird visual and verbal patterns. (*M.A.S.H.* tries to do this, but the design comes out confused, and the effects often cancel each other out.) In the middle of the chaos of a bombardment the dialogue supports this lampoon on war. Harpo is "elected" to serve as a messenger to summon reinforcements by Chico's crooked and odd version of "eenie-meenie-mynie-moe." He is congratulated by Groucho: "You're a brave man! Remember, while you're out there risking life and limb, through shot and shell, we'll be in here thinking what a sucker you are."

The visual and verbal combine in this climactic sequence of *Duck Soup* to give the full dimension of the brothers' chaotic humour. As they march nervously back and forth at the central war headquarters of Fredonia, playing their battle games, their uniforms change from bastardised Revolutionary War uniforms to Confederate Civil War uniforms—then to a British Nineteenth century military suit that looks like a Buckingham Palace guard outfit. When Groucho's attire turns to a Daniel Boone rig, we realise that we are witnessing (by design or intuition) a symbolic burlesque of all wars.

Harpo and Chico are used to advantage by writers Bert Kalmar and Harry Ruby. A first rate director of comedy, Leo McCarey, who served his apprenticeship handling many Laurel and Hardy shorts in the silent and early sound periods, tightens up Chico and Harpo's scenes; he avoids the now standard instrumental solo scenes by these two brothers. In many Marx films the visual and verbal comedy of Chico and Harpo cancel each other out because each of the two comedians often ad libs in a way that suppresses the other's gags.

McCarey shows Chico as the low key, nonchalant spy who has a "what-the-hell" attitude toward his job. His employer, Ambassador Trentino (Louis Calhern), becomes very disturbed with Chico. As the official fusses about a lack of action by his spies, Harpo executes many practical jokes on the ambassador behind his back. The visual plays an important counterpart to the verbal by intruding enough to help maintain the familiar Marx produced chaos but never cancelling out the dialogue.

Visual comedy reigns when Harpo and Chico encounter "slow burn" comedian Edgar Kennedy as the lemonade salesman. Borrowed from old time vaudeville, a confusing three man exchange of hats develops, with Kennedy the object of the attack. A hoary vaudeville routine, to be sure, but the skill with which the three players execute the ancient vignette adds to the fun of the whole picture. Another shade from the popular dumb act of the variety show crops up later in the picture. In an elaborate hiding-impersonation game, Chico and Harpo dress like Groucho. Clad in a night cap and shirt plus cigar, glasses, and mustache, Harpo does a near perfect mirror routine with Groucho. In a scramble the mirror has been broken, so Harpo becomes Groucho's image. Groucho's vanity before a mirror starts the process, but he begins to note that discrepancies exist and tests the image for authenticity. Despite a few lapses in Groucho's perceptiveness (they become gross for comedy's sake) Harpo passes the test until Chico arrives with the same disguise and upsets the playful deception. This "dumb turn" adds to the picture and, like the encounter with Kennedy, proves that the Marx Brothers might have been able to adapt effectively to the silent screen if they had wished to abandon their successful stage career in the Twenties.

Verbal wit in *Duck Soup* was still on a high enough level to keep Groucho the focus of attention. Trapped by an enemy bombardment, Groucho runs to the short wave radio and shouts in desperation:

> Calling all nations! Calling all nations! This is Rufus T. . . . *(He is interrupted by a falling piece of the ceiling and puts on his hat—forgetting to finish his name)* . . . coming to you through the courtesy of the enemy. We're in a mess, we're in a mess! Rush to Fredonia! Three men and one woman trapped in a building. Send help at once! If you can't send help, send two more women. *(Harpo walks in the door and holds up three fingers.)* Make it three more women.

A similar kind of cool expediency with a plea for options manifests itself when Groucho is locked in a bathroom. He screams for help and then observes, "Hey, let me out or throw me a magasine!"

Little needs to be said about the merits of the team's 1935 feature *Night at the Opera*. Critics have hailed it as number one and have sometimes overrated it. Certainly, it ranks either first or second in the Marx series of films, but it does show a return to the use of romantic leads in a parallel or sub-plot position. This technique borrowed from stage musicals would eventually affect the quality of their later works—especially when the sentimental part of the drama equalled or paralleled the more comic one.

Risqué comments by Groucho were still possible in 1935—as if the Marx Brothers had a special dispensation from the Hays Office. When Groucho hears how high the fee of an opera singer is, he makes a suggestion: "You're willing to pay him a thousand bucks a night just for singing. Why I can get a phonograph record of Minnie the Moocher for seventy-five cents. Four a buck and a quarter you can get Minnie." When he sets his sights on Margaret Dumont (again a dowager; this time called Mrs. Claypool), he stretches on her bed and reads a book. Indignantly she inquires, "What will people say?" "They'll probably say you're a very lucky woman," he shoots back. "Now shut up so I can continue my reading."

As would-be agents of singers, Groucho and Chico engage in one of the best two-man vignettes of their career. It beautifully lampoons contracts and legal jargon. "The party of the first part should be known as the party of the first part," says Groucho to a puzzled Chico as he reads a passage from a contract for the second time. Chico notes that it sounds better the second time through. "Well, it grows on you," cracks Groucho. "Would you like to hear it again?"

Night at the Opera has some well-hued gags and routines. Producer Irving Thalberg of M-G-M made the brothers take many of the picture's best scenes on the road as a stage show before the shooting of the film commenced. From this unusual method of developing routines for a motion picture comedy, the crowding of Groucho's closet-like stateroom, a routine that emphasised visual comedy, seemed to profit most.

Both Groucho's and Harpo's autobiographies (*Groucho and Me* and *Harpo Speaks!*) tell about their association with Thalberg and their willingness to change the approach to their story material and cut the number of their gags in half. *Night at the Opera* did seem to prove Thalberg's view because it grossed twice the amount that *Duck Soup* grossed. The producer could be considered an accurate evaluator of the tastes of the period. Cutting the number of gags made the film compatible with the attitudes and the pace of living of the average person of the times. But it may have cut some of the fire and free spirit of the team, though it was not immediately noticeable in *Night at the Opera*. Thalberg's suggestion to reinstate the strong romantic sub-plot was another effective analysis of the taste of the period, but it would soon prove a weakness that affected the total comedy. Also, it should be realised, the Marx Brothers flourished best in an anti-sentimental age, and the tone of the times was changing. The genteel, folksy period had arrived by the middle of the Thirties. Besides this genteel trend the sophisticated comedy also blossomed, employing a humour that often approached high wit. But the brothers did not exist in the worlds of the genteel or the sophisticated. They were alien to both.

A Day at the Races (1937) was the last work of the golden period. Chico achieved one of the great triumphs of his career when he was able, as he occasionally did, to con the con-man. Disguised as an ice cream salesman, he hawked his wares at the racetrack: "Here your tutsi-frutsi! Your ice cream!" Actually, he wanted to find a sucker to buy a library of "dope" books on how to win at horse racing. Groucho became the gullible buyer and had to purchase a second book to decode or interpret the first. Lured from the horse he had originally decided to bet on, Groucho became entangled in the reading of the books he'd obtained from Chico. The race finished before Groucho could decide on a horse, and he discovered that his original choice had won and that Chico had disappeared. Exasperated, Groucho threw his arm load of books into Chico's abandoned ice cream cart and called "tutsi-frutsi" in search of a sucker.

Also effective were the three brothers' actions as quack doctors. They engage in an examination of Margaret Dumont as if they were garage mechanics and barbers. These moments are excellent, but the picture has a lot of dull stretches and some uninspired musical numbers that mark the work several notches below the other Marx films of the golden period.

In their period of decline the Marx Brothers still produced many good scenes. However, the total work never added up to the quality of the works they had created earlier. *Room Service*, released in 1938, has many of the confinements of the stage play on which it was based. Occasionally we see the old Groucho sparkle, but his put-downs seem milder, and there seems no place for his lurking lechery and lust for gold to express itself fully in this mild, fairly well-written dramatic work.

Harpo suffered most in the fade-out. His character seemed to slip into the category of an idiot child who was more disturbing than laughable. However, his ability to "talk" with animals in *At The Circus* (1939) gave him a new dimension that made his "dumb" act with dumb animals intriguing. In this movie Groucho also came forth with a song "Lydia, the Tattooed Lady" by Harold Arlen and E. Y. Harburg that was worth the price of admission.

As they entered the next decade, *Go West* (1940) proved that old comedians don't die; they just fade away. But before their artistic demise they still had the afterglow of the shooting star falling from its zenith. Groucho, the clever one, gets bilked by Chico and Harpo in a train station. When he tries to sell them a shabby coonskin cap and a jacket, he discovers he has met his match and tries to withdraw before he loses everything. The climactic sequence, a race with the Marx Brothers in charge of a locomotive, has its moments, but it is reminiscent of a scene in which Keaton handled similar material more effectively in 1928.

With only three starring features left in their career, *The Big Store* (1941), *A Night in Casablanca* (1946), and *Love Happy* (1949), the brothers added nothing new to their stock in trade. Their efforts in the Forties, like the efforts of Laurel and Hardy, Joe E. Brown, and W. C. Fields, were rather pathetic. The quality of the Marx Brothers' films ranged from mediocre to good when compared with other comedies produced during this period. But the laughter was fading; none of these works came close to the quality of their features produced from 1931-1937, the golden period.

Because there is so much that is good in the worst Marx Brothers' film, there is a natural desire to edit out the dull, the trivial, and the misfired routines that corrupt the whole. In fact, the Marx Brothers' total output prompts the critic to embark on a reconstruction and revision project. A person is inclined to get a hold of the film and "improve" it. If those weak sub-plots using romantic leads could just be scrapped. Such a project would prove more disastrous than the attempt of the Eighteenth century theatre producers, plus some important literary figures, to "improve Shakespeare" by editing and rewriting his works. A play, of course, is a blueprint that can outlive tampering since the original version by the playwright usually survives. A film, however, is the production, and we have found that it may suffer great damage in the hands of even well-intentioned alteration.

Actually, the work of the Marx Brothers needs no apologia. Their films were an interesting blend of vaudeville, stage musical, and silent screen comedy. No other comedy team came close to duplicating their creations. Some similarities to their vaudeville routines can be seen in the routines of such groups as the Ritz Brothers, Clark and McCullough, Wheeler and Woolsey, and, in a way, even the Three Stooges. But all of these teams existed on a much lower artistic scale of achievement. Most of the movies of these teams were pale fare next to a Marx Brothers film of the golden age. The quality of the performance, the material, and the overall spirit of the Marx films were superior. Occasionally a minor team like Wheeler and Woolsey would produce a quality comedy film like *Cockeyed Cavaliers* (1934), but none of the minor groups had the talent to sustain an output of excellent comedies. Only one other major team, Laurel and Hardy, achieved the critical and popular success that would rank them as major comedy stars of the Thirties.

The 1929 *Cocoanuts* employed all four of the Marx brothers, Zeppo, Groucho, Chico, and Harpo.

Groucho woos Thelma Todd in *Horse Feathers* (1932).

Antics of the three brothers in a crowded stateroom
and Allan Jones (next to Harpo) in the 1935 film,
A Night at the Opera.

Harpo uses food as make-up in the dining scene of
A Night at the Opera.

Chico and Harpo get around to harassing Groucho (as they do in most of the brothers' films) in *A Day at the Races* (1937).

The team obviously have designs on Esther Muir in this scene from *A Day at the Races*.

The madcap threesome move in, *Room Service* (1938).

In *Room Service* the zanies enjoy running up a huge bill.

In *At the Circus* (1939) a giraffe takes liking for the ample back of Margaret Dumont.

The quality of their work fades in 1940 as the brothers do their best in *Go West*. Groucho begins his conning activities in this shot.

It doesn't take long for the bilker to be bilked in *Go West*.

5
Duet of Incompetence

Critics and fans often have been impressed by the facile, subtle pantomime of Stan Laurel and are amazed to witness an example of an artful silent screen comedian employing his talents in the sound age. There can be little disagreement among the critics and fans that Laurel's work as a comedian in the Thirties placed him among the notable actors of the period. But sometimes it is not realised that the appeal of his portrayal resulted from its link, indeed, a meshing, a fusing with the character portrayal by the second half of the team, Oliver Hardy. Dialogue and situation in most of the pair's comedies pointed up the strong relationship between the characters enacted. As their career pivoted from its apex and went on a slow downhill slide, a prophetic scene developed in the 1939 production, *Flying Deuces.* Rejected by the girl he loves, Oliver urges Stan to commit suicide with him and becomes indignant with him for wanting to escape the same fate of self-inflicted drowning:

OLLIE: So that's the kind of guy you are. After all I've done for you! Do you realise that after I'm gone you'll just go on living by yourself. People would stare at you and wonder what you are. And I wouldn't be there to tell them. There'd be no one to protect yah. Do you want that to happen to you?
STAN: *(Almost crying)* I never thought of that. I'm sorry if I hurt your feelings, Ollie. I didn't mean to be so dispolite.

In 1940 the team would make two more effective features, *A Chump at Oxford* and *Saps at Sea,* but the relationship of the actors waned with the fading quality of their films.

At the time of their heyday there was no comedy team as unified—one that worked as a perfect duet—in all of motion picture history. This coalescence existed in their character relationship, the story line, and the comic spirit of most of their works. A warm attachment between the two weak, struggling souls made them lovable to the audience. In fact, a revival of interest in Laurel and Hardy evolved in the Sixties. So great has the affection for the team become that a country wide fan club called Sons of the Desert, derived from the title of the team's 1934 feature, has flourished. For these devotees, more than the critics, the characters created by Stanley Laurel and Oliver Hardy are equally important.

A look at the feature films of the team reveals the importance of Oliver Hardy as the actor and as the character he enacted.* Some of their most tightly plotted works, *Sons of the Desert* (1934), *Our Relations* (1936), and *Blockheads* (1938), feature Hardy taking action and functioning as a "plot mover." Laurel was more often a creature of reaction, although he occasionally suggested a plan of action which Ollie would then execute with Stan's help. In *Blockheads,* for example, Stan points out to Ollie that he (Ollie) has been insulted by James Finlayson and should defend his honor. Ollie is moved to action while Stan functions only as a man giving moral support and, of course, Hardy loses the fight. His humiliation produces some of the funniest moments in this film, as it does, generally speaking, in the team's other films.

While Hardy can be said to be the aggressive one who promoted the overall comic entanglements, it must be realised that the two operated as a team in all their works in a way that gave

---

*In all their films Laurel and Hardy employed their own full names. This practice came down from silent times and had almost faded out. It was retained by many one- and two-reel comedians during the thirties.

them a distinction from all other comic teams of the period. Ollie often asked Stan to do a simple task which Stan, the denser member of the team, found too puzzling to solve. Like a frustrated child, he appealed to his friend for help. With an annoyance that occasionally bordered on disgust Hardy would declare, "When you want anything done right, do it yourself," and would then proceed to take over the situation. Of course, he would botch the job, and disaster would rain on him. He became the victim of a simple task which ran amok because of his own slight brain power and some act of Stan's that complicated the situation. Stan, for example, turns on a gas stove and then looks for a match in *Blockheads*. Not able to find a match, he finally appeals to Ollie. Unaware that the stove has been turned on, Hardy lights a match and enters the kitchen. An explosion sends Ollie flying through the air as the bewildered Stan looks at the chaos of the room in shambles, thinking it was caused by an earthquake.

This duet of incompetence seems to have its roots in the past. Ollie is the braggart warrior of Roman comedy whose dignity must be defended with words. He is, however, a coward who must be forced into a fight. Stan often functions as a dim-witted servant, also a character from ancient times—the essence of trusting stupidity and a man who often gets his superior into trouble. There could also be said to be a link with the stand-up comedy teams that used German, Yiddish, Swedish, Negro, and Irish characters in the vaudeville of the Nineteenth century. One member of this type of team was more stupid than the other.

When their first feature, *Pardon Us*, was produced in 1931 by Hal Roach, some of the roots of vaudeville were evident, more so than in any of their succeeding pictures. There are comic vignettes in the schoolroom, minstrel songs, and even a blackface sequence by Laurel and Hardy. These were favourite subjects of the variety show of the Nineteenth century. A screenwriter who created some good silent screen scenarios, H. M. Walker, produced this disjointed work, *Pardon Us,* that handicapped the pair. It was typical of the meandering type of comedy concocted two years earlier as the transition to sound began. Producing works that were released by M-G-M, Hal Roach was manufacturing low-budget pictures with strong ties to past practices. Consequently, many of the early features of Laurel and Hardy had some of the same defects of the two-reeler in the transition to sound period.

Pardon Us has little to recommend it—many negative facets of the picture work against it. Rambling from one routine to another, the story line seems almost non-existent. An attempt to focus the plot on prison life was basically sound, but almost a fourth of the drama takes place in another environment, on a cotton plantation. By placing two mild, cowardly men, arrested for manufacturing beer without a licence, among thugs confined for robbery and murder had potential, but little was made of the comic possibilities. Laurel and Hardy, trying to sleep in an upper bunk, couldn't give sparkle to this routine which had already been done in their first sound picture, a two-reeler called *Berth Marks* (1929). Using James Finlayson as the prison teacher in a scene that was warmed over vaudeville might have promoted more laughter if director James Parrott had had a script to match the talent of the stars. When the plot veered to another environment that contrasted sharply with the picture's attempt to burlesque the popular prison movie *The Big House* (1930) starring Chester Morris and Wallace Beery, the greatest damage to the comedy was done. Laurel and Hardy escape and disguise themselves in blackface. When they are picking cotton with Negroes in the south, the minstrel characteristics of the movie evolve. Ollie sings a number called "Lazy Moon" with a pseudo-spiritual flavour, and Stan does a little comic dance. When they are captured and sent back to prison, no clear line of dramatic development can be seen. Another routine from an earlier picture was employed. This is a dentist chair vignette, also a favourite of vaudeville, which does not seem to belong to the story. Then the pair accidentally thwart a big prison escape. The sequence is not especially comic or exciting enough for a climax. Known to be an expansion of an originally planned short film production, *Pardon Us* clearly shows the paste and patch work that too often plagued the pair's creations.

In a maze of routines some of the qualities of the comedy pair emerge in their first feature. Ollie's affection for Stan is exhibited during their scene in solitary confinement when Ollie shares with Stan his dream of a bucolic existence raising various crops. Hearing the description of the growing of sweetcorn, strawberries, and raspberries on a farm, Stan complains about the last item on

Ollie's list. "Then we'll grow watermelon," Hardy obliges. Stan's naïveté helps promote comedy when he is passed a sub-machine gun by prisoners beginning their attempted jail break. Accidentally Stan presses the trigger and doesn't know how to stop the mechanism. He executes a comic dance of fear to the periodic bursts and the rain of bullets that scatter everyone to places of safety. While the routine is over-extended, Stan's execution of the comic dance is delightful and shows his talent for obtaining comedy from well-developed physical skills.

What could have elevated the entire film to an effective satire or burlesque of authority actually appeared only sometimes in the dialogue —as when the warden, enacted by Wilfred Lucas, welcomed Stan and Oliver as if they were little children who needed a spanking for their illegal brewing of beer. When they are to be released, the same saccharin yet condescending tones enter the warden's voice as he proclaims:

> Begin life anew. Forget this. Let this episode here be just a quietus to be obliterated from your memory. Don't forget I'm your friend . . . Anything I can do to help you where you stopped off, let me know. Call on me anytime.

Stan's brain ticks slowly, and he blurts out a request which will assist the pair to resume where they "stopped off" in their life before prison: "Can we take your order for a couple of cases."

After producing seven short works of mixed quality plus the outstanding, Academy Award winning three-reeler, *The Music Box* (1932), Laurel and Hardy appeared in the feature *Pack Up Your Troubles*. Like the previous feature this 1932 film was episodic. There were really two stories pasted together in the same fashion that often marred their two-reel works. One story shows the two men's inept struggle with army life. Less than half the film in length, this portion has the most laughable scenes, showing their many problems in training and in the war. The second part of the movie describes their attempt to raise the child of an army buddy who was killed in the war and to locate the grandparents. While not always well-developed, the potential for humour in the second portion was more original than that in the first part. Army comedies had been thoroughly exploited by Chaplin, Keaton, and Langdon; consequently, many of the gags seemed derivative. Laughs are promoted when the pair

drop into the wedding of Eddie Smith (the name of the deceased father) and inform a man who looks like a grandfather (Billy Gilbert) that they wish to give him Eddie's baby. The groom is horrified and protests his innocence while the potential father-in-law becomes angry enough to rout Stan and Oliver with a shotgun. Poor Ollie receives a blast in his ample posterior and after choking back his humiliation decides to continue the search for grandparents with one modification: "From now on, we'll telephone."

The comic technique of role inversion, hardly used to advantage in *Pack Up Your Troubles*, was to be more deftly and extensively developed in the two-reeler, *Their First Mistake* (1932). In *Pack Up Your Troubles* this type of humour blossoms from their attempts to take care of the child. Ollie becomes the wife when he nags at Stan for taking a long trek to a Smith Brother's cough drop factory to look for the grandfather. "You can take care of the baby awhile," Oliver complains, "I've got my ironing to do." Stan takes on the fatherly duties of reading to the little girl. Instead of being passively entertained, the child takes over and tells Stan the story, which puts him to sleep—Stan becomes the baby.

Construction of a total film always gave the team trouble. An interview with Hal Roach by Anthony Slide, published in the Spring 1970 issue of "The Silent Picture," a specialised British screen magazine, revealed a view by Roach that while Stan Laurel was an excellent gag man with only Charles Chaplin his superior, Laurel was not a story man who could construct a total dramatic plot. Interviewer Slide noted that *Fra Diavolo* (1933) had "two different stories taking place." Hal Roach's reply indicated an attitude in developing story material that would have particular effect in the fashioning of the operetta-comedy:

> You didn't have to go on for an hour and a half just doing funny things. You just can't be funny that long. Then I went to New York and bought *Babes in Toyland* . . . There was no story, so I wrote the story on the train journey back.

Roach indicated that even though *Fra Diavolo* was a highly successful picture, Laurel did not like the idea that Roach had written the script for *Babes in Toyland* and revised much of the story line, cutting the effectiveness of the original story. What is clear was Roach's tendency to go along with the fad for musical operettas at this time. It became necessary to patch comedy scenes with serious scenes that were similar to the Jeanette MacDonald and Nelson Eddy vehicles like *Naughty Marietta* (1935). Critics and audiences in the Thirties were not as disturbed with the disjointed nature of the script that resulted. *Fra Diavolo* seemed to have greater unity than Stan and Ollie's other excursions into the operetta, *Babes in Toyland* (1934), *The Bohemian Girl* (1936), and *Swiss Miss* (1938). In an age that liked the light opera and did not find the moth-eaten histrionics of the romantic portion of the film merely quaint, the movie proved successful. Some sequences in these films are worthy ones and show the talents of the comedians. In many cases these episodes have been extracted from the total work and released on television today under different titles. Poorly re-titled as *Kidnapped*, for example, was the excerpt from the 1936 *The Bohemian Girl*, with only the comedy scenes retained from the film. In this operetta an elaborate pantomime scene created by Stan wears well with age even though a fantastic gag was employed for the "pay off" or climax of the routine. Stan tried to bottle wine by using a rubber hose as a siphon. He had trouble stopping the flow of wine and problems arranging the bottles and corks, so he merely put the siphon in his mouth. In the process he consumed more wine than he got into the bottles. Very drunk, he mixed up the simple operation in various ways, to promote fine comedy. The final gag revealed a tendency of Laurel to rely on humour that approaches the improbable—a technique seldom employed by silent screen comedians Chaplin, Lloyd, and Keaton. A fantastic gag topped the routine when dazed Stan, with the rubber siphon in his mouth, became so full of his product that it streamed from both his ears.

While the move to produce comic operettas for the musical craze did not provide the unity that so many Laurel and Hardy films lack, the year of the musical, 1933, was also a time when good shorts by the team, *Busy Bodies* and *Dirty Work*, illustrated that with a competent director like Lloyd French, unity could be achieved by focusing the whole story on a work process.

The next year *Sons of the Desert* proved that with a tight scenario by Frank Craven and Byron Morgan plus director William A. Seiter's strong sense of economy in creating a scene, the comedians could create a masterpiece. Evaluator Charles Barr labels it "the most perfect," William Everson calls it "the best and the subtlest," and Leonard Maltin

hails the film as "100% pure Laurel and Hardy."

Today many critics find the musical tangents and the use of disjointed plot material in many of their works injurious to their best comic efforts. The desire for unity may be a fetish of modern criticism, but it has valid roots in basic dramaturgy. A look at other works by major comedians like W. C. Fields and the Marx Brothers show that the films rated highest are the ones that "hold together." It does not mean that some looseness cannot exist in a comedy, but it relates to the necessity for an overall unifying element. This can be achieved by a basic comic idea, a tightly plotted, detailed story line, or characters engaged in a single, simple action that shows a development to a change or a climax. While the last is characteristic of a two-reeler that is effectively plotted, it would seem that *Sons of the Desert* employs all these unifying concepts. The comic idea is concerned with man dominated by his wife; an inversion of the traditional role of man as "one who wears the pants in the family" has been the subject for many domestic comedies. The comic strip "Blondie," starting in the Thirties, uses this theme. W. C. Fields's best films, *It's a Gift* (1934), *The Man on the Flying Trapeze* (1935), and *The Bank Dick* (1940) incorporates this overall, controlling idea.

Sons of the Desert has a detailed plot line which examines various facets of two men's relationships with their wives. Mr. Laurel and Mr. Hardy have wives who are as different as the husbands, but they are both aggressive women. Mrs. Hardy (Mae Bush) resorts to physical violence by throwing dishes and pans when she thinks she has been crossed by her husband; Mrs. Laurel (Dorothy Christie) engages in duck hunting as if she has usurped a man's role and can talk Stan into seeing her way in all matters. There are many scenes that are integral character developing and plot moving segments of the total film; each portion displays a wealth of detailed character and plot material. However, with this complexity there is a single action that assists in unifying the picture. The husbands, like naughty boys, attempt to deceive their wives with the subterfuge that a doctor prescribed a vacation to Honolulu for Oliver's health when, actually, they are going to the Chicago convention of the Sons of the Desert, an organisation that the film burlesques as the Masons and their activities at a Shriner's convention. Such simplicity within complexity makes the work one of the outstanding comedies of the period.

Some of the humorous details in *Sons of the Desert* reveal its richness. In the opening scene the characters of both men are clearly drawn as they react to a solemn, dramatic meeting of the Masonic-like lodge in which the leader gets his group to pledge 100% attendance at a convention. Stan balks at the gravity of the oath, giving his garbled interpretation of the pledge to Ollie, thus planting the essence of the central comic idea:

> The exhausted ruler said that if you took an oath it would have to be broken *(He stumbles on a word as he labours with his slow thought process)* . . . for generations, centuries of hundreds of years. My wife would . . .
> OLLIE: Do you have to ask your wife everything?
> LAUREL: Well, if I didn't ask her, I wouldn't know what she wanted me to do.

Comedy of a bizarre nature develops when Stan sneaks an apple from Mrs. Hardy's fruit bowl. His stupidity becomes apparent as he reads "The American Magazine" and with difficulty tries to masticate the wax fruit. With incredulity and disgust Ollie informs his wife that Stan has been eating "phony fruit." His wife's reply shows that she has had dealings with dim-witted Stan before because she expresses her reaction without amazement: "So that's where it's been going. That's the third apple I've missed this week."

Seldom displaying wit, the dialogue of a Laurel and Hardy work has a functional quality that fits the nature of the characters and the situation. Stan often gets words and phrases confused or takes a statement literally. When Oliver complains to his nagging wife that she's "making a mountain out of a mole hill," Stan joins his pal with the garbled observation, "Certainly, life isn't short enough." Just as Chico Marx did in his films, Stan often substitutes words that jolt the senses: "I think he's suffering a nervous shakedown." When Ollie comes forth with an argument for his freedom to go to the convention, he caps his plea with "All work and no play makes Jack a dull boy." Stan inquires, "Jack who?" Specific word play that approaches high comedy can be witnessed when Ollie complains about the doctor who has been engaged by Stan. By mistake he has procured the services of a veterinarian to treat Hardy. Stanley defends himself with the observation: "Well, I didn't think his religion would make any difference."

Verbal wit in *Sons of the Desert* is more often linked to the situation and to the character than to any of the team's features; there is a successful balance between the visual and the verbal. Here was a fully-fledged sound movie without a vignette that seemed lifted from the silent screen film without refurbishment. Furthermore, there were no routines in the comedy that seemed overdone or repetitive. The control exercised by director Seiter evidently prevented the use of a protracted, monotonous series of gags in any one scene—a fault that is obvious in some Laurel and Hardy movies.

Three other films, *Our Relations* (1936), *Way Out West* (1937), and *Blockheads* (1938) exhibit some of the same virtues of *Sons of the Desert*, but certain faults relegate them to a lower level than the team's masterpiece. Stan Laurel was able to obtain a firmer control of their material by 1936, and while these three works rank above the shorts and features they starred in during 1934 and 1935, some scenes and sequences misfire.

Our Relations has not received a high ranking from modern day critics; nevertheless, it has many qualities that demand a re-examination. Both fans and critics may find this comedy higher on the plus side with the passing of time. It uses the most complicated plot ever employed by Laurel and Hardy. Hal Roach agreed to release the feature as a "Stan Laurel Production," and Laurel employed four writers for adaptation and gags, using W. W. Jacobs's story "The Money Box." The story line goes back to the *Menaechmi* of Plautus and Shakespeare's *Comedy of Errors*. In the film the comedians enact dual roles as they did in *Brats* (1930) and *Twice Two* (1933), which were two-reelers. In the former they play their own sons and in the latter, their respective wives—that is, both play female roles as well as male roles. Trick photography, usually the matte shot, becomes highly important in these two-reelers, but the feature only uses this process in the resolution of the story when the twin brothers meet.

Another dimension of the characters of Stan and Ollie evolves in *Our Relations* when they play the roles of their twin brothers, Al and Nick. These two long lost brothers are sailors by profession and are more aggressive and slightly more intelligent than the standard portrayal of the team. In their devil-may-care attitude toward life and women, Al and Nick contrast sharply with the happily married, docile husbands, Stan and Ollie. As in the precursors of this type of farce, complications develop through the device of mistaken identity. A tavern-restaurant owner (played by Alan Hale) presents a large bill for a meal that Al and

Nick have ordered with two pick-ups who decide
to get the best meal of the house. Naturally, as
a farce plot of this nature goes, the wives meet
the two floosies who mistake their husbands for
Al and Nick. Misunderstandings develop for both
sets of twins, and the wrath of the four women
descends on them. With questionable logic Oliver
concludes that if they are going to be maligned
by the community and harassed by their spouses,
they might as well do the town so that the wives
will really be ashamed of their false accusation.
He thinks this action will bring an apology from
them. Stan agrees, and with a confused metaphor
that indicates unintentionally what will happen
to them says, "We'll give 'em enough rope so
we can hang ourselves." All is eventually resolved
when Stan and Oliver meet their twin brothers,
but not until many more people get involved in
the confusion of identities.

Some critics may find that this elaborate farce
does not help the team. However, Stan and Oliver
reveal the scope of their comic skills, and the
variation on their standard characters provided by
the enactment of Al and Nick seems to give them
a wider gamut of comedy for one feature length
work. The step-up in pace of the show, which
results from complications, also makes the film
more enjoyable to today's audiences in their enthusiasm for rapid fire comedy. The duet has a
tendency to work too slowly at times so that a
comic punch line or a concluding sight gag is
telegraphed to the audience before they get to it.
This pace also has a tendency to eliminate the
overdrawn, repetitive routine that often taints their
work.

The 1937 production, *Way Out West,* probably
has been overrated by critics and fans, but it is
a product of Laurel and Hardy's art at maturation
—a ripeness that lasted from 1933 through 1938.
During this period they also produced many duds
in short and feature length movies. *Bonnie Scot-
land* (1935), for example, was an eight-reel work
that could have been a product of almost any
minor comedy team of the time—teams like
Wheeler and Woolsey or the Ritz Brothers. It
remains one of their most disappointing efforts.
Two other features, *Pick a Star* (1937) and *Swiss
Miss* (1938), are musically based and have many
of the faults of the *genre* without the virtues.

Way Out West contains several musical diversions that some critics find attractive and view as
worthy additions that do not become intrusions.
Laurel and Hardy's soft shoe dance and their

singing of "In the Blue Ridge Mountains of
Virginia" are charming and well executed, but
they do some violence to plot progression by taking
time for a diversion. Nevertheless the picture ranks
high because of the pair's deftness in acting, which
is at its peak. There seems to be proper motivation
for most of their comic scenes. Innovation is seldom lacking. The variety of gags developed in
their attempts to sneak into an upstairs window
of comic villain Finlayson's saloon makes the
picture a very funny one.

Blockheads (1938) was planned as their last
feature. It would have been better for their reputation if they had retired while they were ahead.
Their career started slipping after *Blockheads.*
Their acting talents were now almost flawless,
they were able to control all facets of their comedy
characters, and they had achieved the ability to
get the most from their story material. Exploiting
these assets in *Blockheads,* Laurel and Hardy illustrated how the leading actors themselves could
give unity to a comedy. The desire of Hardy to
help his homeless old war buddy by inviting him
to his house is a character-plot focus that gives
the film cohesiveness. The picture contains many
of the old situations refurbished from previous
pictures, but the touch of Harry Langdon as gag
man for the picture, combined with Stan Laurel's
sense of comedy "bits," gives newness to the old.
A tone of the wistful, sad-faced little clown of
the silents, coupled with Stan's deft mime when
he dumps a huge load of sand over Ollie and his
automobile reveals the influence of a rich heritage.
Stan's legs and body come into play when a minor
gas explosion is mistaken for an earthquake. With
a Langdonesque move of the inquisitive child,
Stan leans against the side of the building to test
its stability, quickly runs away, then stops and
looks back, expecting the large apartment building
to begin collapsing like a house of cards.

In no other feature does Ollie's comedy of
frustration seem more artfully handled. All his
warm, gentlemanly efforts to assist a friend back-
fire. He generally becomes the victim of his own
graciousness. He allows his friend to test the automatic garage door, but Stan misses the driveway
plate that trips the mechanism and ploughs
through the door, running Ollie down and de-
molishing the automobile. As Oliver first catches
sight of Stan, he finds his buddy seated in a wheel
chair with his leg folded under him. Thinking
that Stan has lost a leg in the war, he caps one
of their best dark humour situations by correcting

a statement and thereby emphasising his inept attempt to be polite. Inviting him home for a dinner, Ollie oozes courtesy and charity: "Wait until you put your legs under that table . . . *(Pauses and smiles nervously, starting over)* Pardon me. You just wait until you put your leg under that table . . ." The humour was considered too sharp and crude for the tastes of the late Thirties, but in our present day enthusiasm for dark and anti-sentimental humour, we find this type of comedy delectable.

Viewed today, the declining period of Laurel and Hardy, like that of the Marx Brothers and W. C. Fields, is painful to those who love their best works. The old fire and the zip emerge only occasionally during the pair's decline. *A Chump at Oxford* and *Saps at Sea,* created in 1940, are good works. Slow moving and even dull scenes affect the total, but they are still two respectable movies that rank high when compared to the total output of the team and to other comedies of 1940. The laughter from the audience began to fade in 1941 when they moved from Roach's domain and made nine more films—mostly for 20th Century-Fox and M-G-M.

When Laurel and Hardy began dealing directly with the major studios, their artistic demise was assured. Roach had an indirect relationship with M-G-M when the team began making sound pictures in 1929; in 1940 Roach released his productions through United Artists. Stan Laurel, like many silent screen stars of the Twenties, had a great deal of control over their work. Roach gave him even more control in 1936 and the label "Stan Laurel Productions" appeared on three excellent features, *Our Relations, Way Out West,* and *Blockheads.* By 1941 the team had to abandon its working method. They had little control even though their pictures had been very popular. The mills of the big studios were quite different from those of the relatively smaller studio. The assembly line technique in shooting a movie often relegated the stars to the status of mere cogs in the huge machine.

By 1940 Laurel and Hardy had already produced features that exhibited the tell-tale signs of decline. But the big studio systems of 20th Century-Fox and M-G-M completely drained the enthusiasm they had for their art. By this time they needed the spark of major comic writers and directors, but the studios treated them as property, as if they were working in B pictures. One of the most talented directors they worked with was Sam Tay-

lor, who had assisted Harold Lloyd to his fame in the Twenties. Nevertheless, *Nothing But Trouble* which he directed for them in 1944 was weak. The title was one that might be applied to their last, laboured efforts.

At the zenith of their career Laurel and Hardy were incomparable. No other cinema team worked the same way to achieve comedy or created characters with as much dimension. This distinctiveness gives them a place in film history. While they employed many slapstick scenes often executed by pasteboard, mechanical comedians of their age, they evolved characters of warmth—a warmth that has never been equalled by another comedy team. It is easier to compare the blatant robot activities of a Clark and McCullough, a Wheeler and Woolsey, an Olsen and Johnson, and the Ritz Brothers with the Marx Brothers. The glib, automatic routines of these teams, however, place them on the cooler side of the Marx Brothers. Not only were the Marx Brothers better artists; they displayed a cameraderie that often burned brightly and a flair in their characterisations that made them appealing and likeable. But they were never lovable to audiences in the same way that Laurel and Hardy were. Great comedians touch more than the funnybone; they find a way to the heart. We can see general humanity and even ourselves, specifically, mirrored in their portraits. Something universal in characterisation will make the superior actor's productions live for decades. At the risk of overrating Laurel and Hardy, I believe their films will be appreciated even more in two or three decades than they are now. After all, *Sons of the Desert* approaches its fortieth birthday, and admiration of its qualities grows with the passing of time.

Some say that Abbott and Costello are a comedy team that will be appreciated more in the future. The prospect seems unlikely. These comedians of the Forties lacked the skills demanded of the comic art and the humanity to give their portraits a long life. Viewing their works today, a writer comes to the conclusion that this team never developed characters—they remained merely actors playing a part. Occasionally, a spark of humanity comes from the little, tubby Costello, but his brash companion, Abbott, remains a cold fish. He obviously learned his feeble skills without a love of his art—a glib stand-up, wise guy who might have been better cast as a comic villain. He appears to be the most sadistic straight man in the business when he evolves humour by belittling a stooge who is trusting, struggling dummy. Some will say that this is the point of the comedy, but as a team Abbott and Costello impress only the few who like the material they use without demanding the best from the comic art. The relationship of Laurel and Hardy, on the other hand, is the bond of two struggling, inferior men whose everyday life is plagued with obstacles. Their plight promotes laughter and evokes a degree of sympathy which exceeds that accorded all other comedy teams. Time will prove that they deserve a rank with Chaplin, Lloyd, Keaton, W. C. Fields, and the Marx Brothers.

A publicity shot of the famous team, Laurel and Hardy, made in 1936.

The use of simple material—sailors meet girls—in a 1929 sound, two-reeler, *Men O' War*.

The sailors try to entertain on fifteen cents in *Men O' War*. James Finlayson mans the soda fountain.

On a road gang in *Hoosegow* (1929), a two-reel film.

In the two-reeler *Brats* (1930), Laurel and Hardy enact the roles of their own sons using oversized sets and props.

As itinerant musicians in *Below Zero* (1930), two-reels.

As domestic types, Stan and Ollie in *Our Relations*
(1936).

Our Relations incorporates the team's twins, Al and
Nick, to create comic complications.

Stan and Ollie have a night on the town with a
drunk to defy their wives in *Our Relations*.

In *Way Out West* (1937) the team are lost in the world of "he-men."

A fight for the deed in *Way Out West* with Sharon Lynne and James Finlayson.

Hardy is nearly driven out of his mind testing the product in *Saps at Sea* (1940).

Adrift, they are lost souls in *Saps at Sea*.

"Another fine mess" at the conclusion of *Saps at Sea*.

6

Joe E. Brown and Other Minor League Comedians

In *Fireman Save My Child* (1932), *Elmer the Great* (1933), and *Alibi Ike* (1935) Joe E. Brown was a bush league baseball player with phenomenal talent as a pitcher or a hitter. His character possessed a giant ego concerning these skills but had all the *naïveté* of a country bumpkin. This rube appeared to be easy prey for crooks and a shady lady when he arrived in the big city to play in the major league. However, he not only defeated, by pluck and luck, the villain who plagued him; he won the game and the hand of the little girl back home.

Although Brown exhibited many of the attributes of a major league comedian, critically, his works remain in the minor league of the comedy film. But he nearly made the "big time" with a few excellent comedies that almost place him in the class of W. C. Fields and the comedy teams, Laurel and Hardy and the Marx Brothers. Mr. Brown had a charm and a magnetism that only great comedians possess. But the acid test, the films themselves, do not appear as funny today as they did when they were first created. It takes several decades to judge comic films accurately and, unfortunately, with all their good qualities, Brown's movies have faded slightly—enough to be disturbing to fans who remember the comedian with the fondness of a nostalgic middle-ager.

Probably the key failing in Brown's work is lack of innovation—especially the development of strong gags. All the major comedians of the Thirties, Fields, the Marx Brothers, and Stan Laurel were excellent innovators who developed splendid jokes for their films. The same can be said of silent screen comedians Chaplin, Lloyd, Keaton, and Langdon. True, all these men obtained assistance from hired gag writers, and their directors usually understood the value of excellent comic situations and specific jokes. But the kings of comedy knew what routines or comic "bits" fit their character best. Only when they were fading in their abilities (which might have included their judgement as well as their spirit) did the weakness in gag invention plague them. Joe E. Brown's pictures have the vital, warm comedy character he created but not enough superior gags to create a masterpiece by the critical standards used to measure a classic of film comedy.

Two other aspects worked against Brown and kept him from fulfilling his potential. His ability to control the level of comic overstatement was faulty; at times he overacted a scene by playing it too heavily. Relying on the success story of the genteel comic tradition, the type of material Lloyd and Keaton blended with clever slapstick gags, Brown used an approach that did not always fit the story. With his broader style he appeared to be waiting for more farcical events to transpire. At times he seemed to be "knocking himself out," exaggerating, even in the sentimental, light scenes with a sweet, young girl. Even at the climax, few of his films except *Earthworm Tractors* (1936), have the inventive, rapid-fire gags that were typical of some of the best comedy teams.

Successful in vaudeville and musical comedy, Brown began his career in 1928 by playing in essentially serious pictures that had only a few comic scenes. By 1930 he had his first starring role in *Painted Faces* and, then, star billing in *Hold Everything*. For this latter work Warner

Brothers gave him $15,000. Since he was doing three to five pictures a year, the comedian felt that he had finally achieved the status of a leading actor. It took only one year and a favourable audience response for his pictures to boost his rate per picture to $100,000.

Since Brown had taken the role of a comic pugilist—a role created by Bert Lahr—for the stage version of *Hold Everything,* a critical review that favoured Brown's portrait touched off a battle of words between vaudeville performers. Bert Lahr took offence to Sid Silverman's review in "Variety" and wrote a letter accusing Brown of stealing his own comic character. Brown claimed that he remained in the background and let others speak for him. In his autobiography, *Laughter Is a Wonderful Thing,* written in 1956, Brown described old-time Dutch comedian Sam Sidman's answer to Lahr's letter:

> He gave him hell for claiming anyone could steal what he, Lahr, didn't own. And he went on to say that Lahr had seen him many times and Lahr's makeup and everything he did in the play was taken from Sidman. "And I don't claim any credit for originating the character because I stole it from Sam Bernard," another well known Dutch comedian of a previous era. "I admit it, why don't you?" he asked.

Brown reveals here one of the basic problems of the histrionic art. Actors and critics fall into the same trap when they try to judge others by the criterion of originality. So much in this art is passed down from generation to generation—this includes the material, the technique, and the final form given to the comedy by the actor. Evaluators have to settle for the *execution* by the performer and that added dimension he gives the material through his personality and his use of the tools of his trade.

Hold Everything, while it was Joe E. Brown's important step to success, was not the type of film that would make him a contender for a comedian's crown. According to Mordaunt Hall in the "New York Times," the piece has too many "romantic moments" and "pleasant songs" that were intrusions. Obviously the work was too tied to the vaudeville and musical comedy format. He fared better in comedy that avoided these influences.

One of the better early films with Brown was scripted by Elliott Nugent, a stage playwright and actor who became an important movie director in the Thirties. The plot of *Local Boy Makes Good* (1932) is sound, and the characterisation of the comic protagonist gave the comedian a worthwhile vehicle. A college picture, it probably would have suited Harold Lloyd even better than Brown. In many ways the script was a rehash of the silent screen comedian's *The Freshman* (1925). Since Lloyd was creating his best sound picture in 1932, *Movie Crazy,* he was still in the running. If he had played the leading role in *Local Boy Makes Good,* the overall quality of the work probably would have been much stronger. Nevertheless, Brown does one of his best jobs in portraying a meek social outcast trying to become popular by engaging in athletics. Nugent gives the character some of the standard mannerisms of this comic type—a bookworm with glasses who goes by his full name, John Augustus Miller, and is afraid of his own shadow. But Nugent gives this stock character some insight into his own problem, thus adding dimension. Of his lack of social acceptance John states sadly, "I guess I'm not the kind of fellow people wave at. They just point at me." This observation is directed to Ann, a girl who works in the same bookstore he does—a little store just off the campus. Two girls, Ann and Julia, see him as a subject for moulding. They urge him to become more outgoing and engage in athletics. Julia, who has had a class in psychology, decides to use her version of psychiatry on him: "First, you must tell me all your sexual problems." She ends her session with the poor fellow on the floor, held down by her foot placed aggressively on his chest. Her final advice is a garbled view of developing will power; he must, she maintains, turn his libido from the inside to the outside.

Many good lines plus a climactic track race sequence provide opportunities for Brown to develop comedy. To remove his fear of competition, Ann makes John Miller drink a concoction that is nearly straight alcohol. John ends by running the relay race fully inebriated and yelling "Whoopee, I'm on wings!" Possessing more than average speed under normal conditions, John finds that he can run faster than anyone else even when he is running backwards—that is, facing his opponents but going the same direction. It's a fantastic gag, to be sure, but executed well enough by back screening and a matte shot to make the sequence funny.

In Brown's three baseball pictures previously mentioned, the comedian developed fully his comic portraits. *Elmer the Great* (1933) is one of his prime comedies—among the top four of his films.

Starring in this drama written by Ring Lardner and George M. Cohan for the stage, Joe E. Brown returned to the theatre to boost his morale because he found that the lack of audience reaction in the film medium was adversely affecting the development of his skills. On the stage he depended on audience response to season Elmer's character. Since he had played professional baseball and continued to observe many of the colourful personalities in that sport, he was able to sketch a convincing Elmer, a sleepy-eyed, naïve, small town ballplayer who has superhuman talents on the diamond. Elmer also possesses an independent spirit that cannot be moulded; he is a man who must be constantly humoured, or he may refuse to apply his skills in the middle of a game. He never realises his social ineptitude and, in some situations (especially with a woman), he seems very humble. After winning a game under the pressure of great odds, he indicates a realisation of his own nature in a speech over the radio. Elmer, using his strong twang, announces:

> Trouble is, a bashful guy like I has got to make it look difficult; otherwise, people don't believe yah. I could go on for hours talkin' about myself and how I done it, but I always say that a fellow shouldn't brag about himself. I always make it a rule never to take no credit. And, in closing I want to tell you followers of the Chicago Cubs that yah don't have to worry about the pennant next year as your old friend Elmer Kane will be out there on the field in a Cub uniform.

The screen version of *Elmer the Great* does well in moments like this—scenes from the stage play, but the picture has little to recommend it when it comes to the climactic game. There are not enough fresh gags to make the sequence a high point of the picture.

Filmed one year earlier, *You Said a Mouthful* (1932), a comedy focusing on the sport of long distance swimming, has more cinematic qualities than *Elmer the Great*. In this film more laughs are obtained by a farcical plot in which the protagonist is pushed into a sport at which he is a rank amateur. Because of many accidents that gain him time or actually pull him along in the water when he gets caught by a fish hook and line, he achieves victory, the winner of the long swim. Again he reverts to a Harold Lloyd type of character who wins by pluck and luck. He swims with glasses on in much the same way that Lloyd played football with glasses in *The Freshman*. At the end of the race Joe declares to the crowd: "It was a push-over. I'm not even breathing hard.

In fact, I'm not breathing at all." He turns pale and collapses.

Portraying the struggling salesman, Alexander Botts, rather than an athlete in *Earthworm Tractors* (1936), Brown created the outstanding comedy film of his career. The movie evolved from material suggested in the "Saturday Evening Post" stories of William Hazlett Upson. In creating his twenty-fourth sound feature, Brown once more used the success story in a comic vein instead of the serious tone of the rags to riches novel of Nineteenth century writer, Horatio Alger, Jr. Success in athletic endeavours had become overworked by the mid-Thirties, and a turn to the labour of an eager young man to sell tractors had a freshness in theme that was needed in the cinema. This theme had been used before but mostly in the genteel comedies of the Twenties. By returning to material of the past a renewed look at the old subject matter sometimes brings a fresh perspective especially if one type story material has saturated the public and gone stale.

Writers also usually gain renewed vigour when they move away from the standard work of the period. Edward Macauley, Joe Traub, and Hugh Cummings produce a tight script that has some of the fine characteristics of the well-constructed films of Keaton and Lloyd in their best years, the Twenties. Ray Enright, a former gagman for Mack Sennett, also proves that a comic writer turned director can influence things for the good. *Earthworm Tractors* has excellent gags—the most outstanding of any of Brown's pictures. Enright also seems to know how to handle the comedian in order to get a lively, spontaneous performance from him.

Alexander Botts is a *braggadocio* with more eagerness and less talent than the baseball bumpkins. After seeing his printed card which exalts his abilities as "A Natural Born Salesman and Master Mechanic," the audience soon learns that Alexander is not the formidable person that he would like others to think he is. Since he doesn't know how to operate the huge tractors (tank-like monsters used for road building, not farming), his demonstrations usually end in disaster. Fences and houses get smashed, and a truck gets crushed to a flat, pulpy mass. But like the stereotype of the ever hopping salesman, he has determination and persistence. After being literally thrown out many times by Sam Johnson (Guy Kibbee), he sells a fleet of tractors to this antagonist and marries his daughter.

While *Earthworm Tractors* often exploits material used by the sentimental comedy, it more often ridicules it. The girl Alexander has left back home in the small town gets married to a worthless man who is cynical and soon tired of marriage. Back for a visit, Alexander exhibits shock and extreme sadness when he learns of the union from the shiftless husband. In old-fashioned, melodramatic tones the eager young man who is now apparently crushed observes, "It is better to have loved and lost . . ." he begins, and his rival finishes the statement sourly, ". . . than never to have loved at all." Botts then retorts, "There's always the river . . ." and takes the bouquet he has bought and sadly walks away. No one seems to care what he might do. He suddenly snaps out of his despondency and runs away very happy. A comic reversal caps the gag, and we suddenly realise that he has been going through a ritual; he's glad to have shed the girl back home because he's fallen for Mabel Johnson.

Comic ingenuity, a character trait often used by silent screen comedians, springs forth in several scenes of *Earthworm Tractors*. Faced with a problem of communicating his sales pitch to the hard of hearing Sam Johnson, Alexander prepares a series of signs pinned inside his suitcoat, hat, and the seat of his pants. Asked the price of his product, he opens one side of his suitcoat to reveal a sign reading "$4850 FOB." When Sam asks, "Your tractor any good at road building?" he opens the other side of the coat to show the inscription, "And How!" The pay-off gag finally comes when Alexander is asked the horsepower of the machine. He bends over and lifts his coat tails to reveal the sign "Horsepower 83.23" on his rear.

Visual gags with a tractor are reminiscent of the films of Keaton and Lloyd. Besides the many accidents which Botts has with the machine, he also gets into a jam when he tries to prove how strong the tractor is by using it to tow Sam Johnson's house to a proposed new location. He does this without knowing that Sam and his daughter are still in the house. Stalled on a railroad track, the house, along with its occupants, comes close to being demolished, but Alexander gets it moving again before the onrushing train arrives at the crossing. More elaborate development of this type of "thrill" comedy culminates when Alexander and Sam are travelling in the tractor on the side of a mountain being dynamited in the process of road excavation. A demonstration of the Earthworm Tractor under such hazard conditions becomes effective comedy. A reversal caps the conclusion of this climactic sequence. The explosions cure Sam of his deafness, but Alexander nearly loses his hearing. The black nature of this type of comedy becomes lighter when Mabel arrives, embraces Alexander, and exclaims "Darling!"—glad, of course, that he is now safe from danger. Botts, like the father used to do, asks her to speak up because he doesn't understand her. The father gruffly comes to her aid by repeating the term of affection with cynicism, but showing his grudging acceptance of a worthy, temporarily deaf candidate for a son-in-law.

Time may prove that Joe E. Brown *was* one of the major comedians of the Thirties. *Elmer the Great* and *Earthworm Tractors* are strong, vital slices of Americana that may be discovered by European critics who find Harold Lloyd's portrait of a "young man going up" an important contribution to our comic spectrum. The spoof of the success story in the cinema of the Twenties and Thirties has important sociological implications. Since this theme becomes increasingly sharper in its humorous treatment, veering away from the serious handling of a story that features a poor, bright, young man achieving a high financial status and happiness typical of popular Nineteenth century literary works, the lampoon tends to be corrective. That is, the financial success myth, once used as an ideal, becomes the subject of ridicule. It can be argued, of course, that Harold Lloyd's and Joe E. Brown's use of such lampoons was too light in tone—that their execution never reached the level and, consequently, the sting of satire, a comic form with corrective values more powerful than those found in a simple burlesque.

Starring in over thirty features within a ten year period, Joe E. Brown turned out films that display an unevenness that stems from overproduction. The system's mass production concept probably hurt other comedians of the period. The major comedians of the Twenties who achieved both popular and critical acclaim usually produced their own works. They slowed the pace and took more care in the total creative process. Chaplin, Lloyd, and Keaton keenly felt the pressures that helped them maintain the quality of their films through the decade. Ego was a factor, but they had the pride of an artist who gets satisfaction only from achieving the best of which he is capable.

While the criticism that the "Hollywood system" damages the individual artist has been an oversimplification used by many evaluators, it does explain at least part of the difficulties encountered by comedians in the Thirties. Public demand for its weekly supply of light entertainment promoted hurried, sloppy production. Consignment writing, directing, and acting was the rule of the day, and a contracted artist of the medium had little time to develop his talents. He did the best he could do under the system that required only hack skills from him. Some creative people protested, but most were grateful that they had employment in a time and age that was not noted for its concern with the fine arts. Miraculously, the Thirties produced more excellent character actors and comedians than we have today.

Vaudeville and the musical comedy supplied some seasoned character actors like Leon Errol, who displayed many of the facets of a major comedian. The warmth of his portrayals equalled Joe E. Brown's. This contender for a comedy crown never seemed to get strong enough material to make his pictures rank with the movies of Fields, Laurel and Hardy, and the Marx Brothers. With sixteen features to his credit in the Thirties, he enjoyed an increase in popularity during the Forties when the major comedians were fading. He appeared in twice as many films at this time as he had previously, but all of these features are best forgotten. Some of his two-reelers, *The Jitters* (1938), *Gem Jams* (1943), and *High and Dizzy* (1950), remain better testaments of his talent. Too often in his features he was given a secondary role and slight material.

Errol looked promising in 1930 in *Saps Don't Work* when he posed as a detective to cover up his obsession as a kleptomaniac. Critics recognised his abilities in that age, but he seemed to be a victim of the star system. He often played a supporting comic for Paramount and a character actor for any assignment. Despite the overall weaknesses of the "Spitfire" and "Joe Palooka" series in the Forties and Fifties, a person now over thirty years old may have etched in his memory the beautiful rubber-legged drunk routine and the blustering, sputtering Lord Basil Epping character that proved Errol's craftsmanship as an artist of humour.

Another comedian of the Thirties (and the Twenties) who had great potential but whose talents were not fully extended by studios, writers, and directors, was Charlie Chase. He, like Errol, seems to be more firmly characterised in two-reelers. Chase, for example, was the plot mover and focus for all comedy in such little gems as the 1937 short film, *The Wrong Miss Wright*. He played supporting roles in the features, *Sons of the Desert* (1934) starring Laurel and Hardy and *Kelly the Second* (1936) starring Patsy Kelly. The latter film was typical of so many movies of its kind. With a limited bag of tricks Patsy Kelly managed to mug her way through many two-reelers and over twenty features in the Thirties. A brash, young lady with tom-boy traits in *Kelly the Second*, she serves as a trainer for a prizefighter. She provides some broad comedy as she gets involved in a man's world. The most skilled acting in the motion picture, however, can be seen in Charlie Chase's Doc Klum. Deftly, the actor produces excellent scenes of comic pretension and frustration. Bragging about his pugilist, Cecil Callahan (Guinn "Big Boy" Williams), Doc gets involved with gangster Ike Arnold (Edward Brophy) who fixes fights. It may be that Chase's "fall guy" portrait— a man who is on the receiving end of the joke— was not the kind of characterisation which writers could use as a protagonist. Perhaps, too, the personality may not have had enough box-office appeal for the studios to place him as a lead in features. But, looking with the perspective of a critic three decades removed, I wish they had at least tried.

Another player for the Roach studios who had acted in silent screen comedy, Edgar Kennedy also remained a bit and supporting actor during his long career. In the Thirties he appeared in many two-reelers for RKO—a series, "Average Man" comedies, often displayed the comedian embroiled in a domestic crisis. This crisis usually wasn't much, but a minor problem often mushroomed to giant proportions. Kennedy was even a better "fall guy" than Chase. While Chase portrayed a fussy, easily cowed man next door, Kennedy played the ox who would butt his head against a stone wall. His boob next door could easily get into hot water because he made a simple task into a Herculean effort. He struggled as hard as Laurel and Hardy. Like Hardy he always pretended to know how to do something when he didn't have the faintest idea what he was doing. Consequently, the act of cutting down a tree became a disaster— the tree would end up crushing his own house. Then, his trademark would cap the situation— Kennedy would execute his famous "slow burn" by running his hand over his bald head and down his face, a thoroughly humiliated, angry man.

In a class with Leon Errol, Charlie Chase, and Edgar Kennedy, comedian Billy Gilbert became well-known for his excitable, sometimes fussy paranoid. In *Million Dollar Legs* (1932) he played on his famous sneeze, a gimmick that was repeated in many of his succeeding pictures. Humour derived from the delay and agony caused by this minor personal discomfort. An approaching sneeze evolved slowly and fizzled out only to erupt after it appeared to have been stifled. In *Million Dollar Legs* W. C. Fields assists the comic nature of the routine by his disgusted reaction to this unfortunate man's affliction. Because of this curious means of gaining comedy, Gilbert served as the voice for one of the dwarfs, Sneezy, in *Snow White and the Seven Dwarfs* (1938).

Billy Gilbert's talents were, of course, not confined to a tricky sneeze. He proved to be an excellent heavy for many Laurel and Hardy films. In *Pack Up Your Troubles* (1932) he plays a bit as the angry father-in-law who takes after the two hapless souls with a shotgun; he engages in the same action as the jealous husband (a supporting role) in their 1938 *Blockheads*. However, he was not confined to playing the foil of this famous comedy team. He appeared in over forty features during the Thirties, and in Chaplin's *The Great Dictator* (1940) he appeared as a burlesqued version of Nazi Germany's Goering.

A much different type of comedian than those previously discussed needs some mention as an actor who made strong contributions to the comedy film. Arthur Lake developed a young, insecure, bumbling, almost demented character in many of his bit roles in the Thirties. As an elevator operator and bellboy, for example, he added spice to the sophisticated comedy, *Topper* (1937) by providing some of the broader comedy of frustration. The next year he became a star as Dagwood Bumstead in the first dramatisation of the comic strip "Blondie." He continued to play the role until 1950—a total of twenty-eight features for the "Blondie" series. Lake was a limited actor with a slight bag of comic techniques, but he had a firmness, a consistency, and a flair for the role that made him appealing. True to the comic strip character, his Dagwood showed that Blondie knows best and that he would bungle every task which his boss, Mr. Dithers (generally played by Jonathan Hale), gave him. As a running gag for the movie series, Dagwood was inevitably late to work, and in streaking out of his front door he would predictably collide with the mailman who never knew how to avoid the encounter even though he knew it was to happen. The clash of the two men brought a rain of letters from the sky just

as surely as accumulated objects would fall from Fibber McGee's closet on the radio shows and in the movies created by Fibber and Molly.

Comedy during the depression years had more sparkle because of the charm of the two vaudeville and musical comedy headliners, Bert Lahr and Jimmy Durante. Projecting the eccentric behavior of odd balls who put on airs but who are obviously low-brows from culturally deprived backgrounds, these two comics often lampooned the pretender in all of us. Yet, in the ethos of this type of creature was a universal glow that was captivating—they radiated warmth. Lahr recognised the importance of empathy in creating comedy:

A good comedian has to be a good actor. And the reason for a comedian being a good comedian, he creates a sympathy. He immediately creates a warmth in his audience. (from an interview in *Actors Talk About Acting*, Avon Books, 1961, p. 168).

In *Always Leave Them Laughing* (1949) Lahr appeared as the old vaudeville comedian who tries to teach the young stand-up comedian, played by Milton Berle, how to capture the heart of the audience—a necessity the veteran pointed out, for obtaining "true" comedy. In several old sketches from burlesque used in the film, Lahr proved that he could hold an audience in his palm with a lovable characterisation, but the brash Berle, contrary to the script's conclusion, did not learn from the master—Milton remained the obnoxious, heavy-handed night club comedian who performed mechanical, soulless routines. While Bert Lahr never succeeded in the movies, he made a contribution to the comedy in many colourful bit parts in the Thirties. He also starred in a number of two-reelers, but most of them show hasty production and poor writing. His crowning achievement was, of course, his portrait of Cowardly Lion in the 1939 production of *The Wizard of Oz.**

An equally lovable comedian, Jimmy Durante was paired with Buster Keaton in the early Thirties. Durante seemed headed for star billing, but he projected an eccentric type of character that seemed more suited to a supporting or bit role. The most durable of the old timers, he was an excellent supporting actor for Donald O'Connor in *The Milkman* (1950). When you look at this slight, contrived work today, you realise that

---

*See Chapter Three for an analysis of the film and Bert Lahr's contribution. For interesting reading consult *Notes on a Cowardly Lion*, a biography of Lahr by his son John.

Durante stole the show from O'Connor without effort. The young comedian "knocked himself out" as Jimmy sailed through his part with all the charm of an old pro (he was sixty when he made this film) who knew how to make the best of a comic situation. Appearing in movies, vaudeville, night clubs, and radio, Durante may have spread his talent too thin. Unfortunately, the comedian does not have a single movie to his credit that can be placed in the top rank of film comedies. As it failed to do with Bert Lahr, Hollywood never realised his fullest potential.

Odd as it may be, while the movie industry seemed to slight some of the potentially great film comedians, it often doted on actors from vaudeville and the musical comedy who lacked the charisma of Lahr and Durante. Besides this deficiency, the Hollywood establishment frequently worked with inferior material and its performances were merely workmanship jobs. The comedy team, Bert Wheeler and Robert Woolsey, for example, produced strong individual comedy scenes in their films, plus one good feature, *Cockeyed Cavaliers* (1934), that still have merit when viewed today. But most of their motion pictures were almost as routine as the two-reelers of Bobby Clark and Paul McCullough. In *Kickin' the Crown Around* (1933) this pair spouted vaudeville patter that might have been funny when first screened, but routines of this nature now merely seem quaint. Clark and McCullough had the technical skill of an excellent comedy team, but they limited themselves to gags that did not support and develop solid comic characterisations.

To create lasting humour, I believe the screen comedian must focus on the building of a portrait that fits his personality and his skills. The pitfall of many screen clowns seems to have been their reliance solely on a farcical plot or on gag material like that used by run of the mill night club comedians. To accentuate the problem, the screen (including television), is a cool medium that does not allow the full development of empathy. In a live performance there is a magical bond between the player and the audience. Reaction from the viewer is not merely a stimulus; the interplay between performer and onlooker becomes an integrated whole—it becomes the show. The movie comedian, therefore, has a greater task. He must transmit to the cameras a portrait that bridges the gap between a life performance and a reproduction of a performance. The mechanics of the

comedy profession suffer the most in front of that objective, frigid eye of the camera.

The best example of the mechanics of the art can be found in the Three Stooges. There may be something camp or nostalgic in their wild activities that gives them appeal in some quarters, but I find them a degeneration of the fine art of slapstick. This trio uses the silent screen art (the dialogue is so inconsequential that the sound might as well be confined to non-verbal effects), and in their hands, it seems to be an inferior form. Seldom are gags properly motivated. There are many scenes that consist of poking each other's eyes, hammering on a head, or twisting a nose—a strange orgy of attack provoked by a slight misunderstanding. When Bud Abbott and Lou Costello entered movies in the Forties, they assisted in the decline of the silent screen art of slapstick. Since the Three Stooges made shorts from the Thirties into the late Fifties, it now may be seen that the team did not have the excuse of being on the tail end of a great tradition. Their earlier works are not much better than their last films. They didn't suffer the fade-outs of the leading comedians of the period. To put it bluntly, at the risk of offending Three Stooges fans, they never were talented comedians. They lacked the spark, the innovation, and the freshness to place them even in the front ranks of the minor comedians.

Although it has seldom been realised, because the complicated activities and fevered production of the times have obscured the details, comeback attempts were made in the Thirties. Popular comedians of the past struggled once more to gain a foothold, but they all failed.

Roscoe "Fatty" Arbuckle, after a scandal that forced him from stardom in the early Twenties to the obscurity of minor directing jobs under an assumed name, returned to leading roles in two-reelers. Warner Brothers, under the subsidiary corporation, Vitaphone, starred him in *Hey Pop* in 1932, *Buzzin' Around, How've You Been,* and *Tomalio* in 1933. This last two-reel film was a broad farce set in a South American location. Director Ray McCarey, creator of Hal Roach shorts and a Laurel and Hardy feature, *Pack Up Your Troubles* (1932), did little to help Fatty with his comeback. A poverty of gag invention plagued this cheaply made two-reeler. Also the comedian lacked the vocal skills to handle the sound medium. In the climactic sequence of this piece, crude humour evolves from showing an obese man engaging in a foot race. With such weak works Arbuckle didn't have a chance, but if he had been able to recoup from such ventures, he might have been a star again. Unfortunately, his efforts were cut short by his death in 1933.

Even more curious was the appearance of a vaudeville team that started in the late Nineteenth century. Somewhat successful on radio, Joe Weber and Lew Fields tried their hand at the talkies for Standard Motion Pictures in New York. They starred in the now obscure work, *Beer Is Here*, a 1931 featurette (over two reels but under five). The vaudeville patter of the team, generally in a German or Dutch dialect, never caught the fancy of the movie public. They remained as curiosities of the past.

In the same pattern of reviving the past, Vitaphone dipped into the 1910s with a re-creation of Mack Sennett's Keystone Kops. This odd item, *Keystone Hotel* (1935), was directed by Ralph Staub and displayed a collection of aging silent comedians along with a star of serious feature works of the past, Marie Prevost. Ford Sterling once more played his Dutch comic chief of police, and Hank Mann enacted a house detective. Ben Turpin tried his hand as Count Drewablank, a fashion expert, while Chester Conklin became the indignant husband whose wife is wooed by Sterling. A disjointed screenplay by Joe Traub attempted a revival of the early slapstick of the silent screen. The climactic episode had both an orgy of pie throwing at a fashion show and a rush of the police to stop this conflict among the supposed sophisticated set. A wild scurry to the scene of the action becomes an imitation of the Keystone Kops, and a collection of troubles beset the police—all in accelerated motion. When the police finally arrive, Sterling, as the chief, bellows: "Stop in the name of the law!" The pie splashed crowd turn on him, and he becomes the target—a deluge of pies leave him buried in pastry. The topper to this gag (as if this weren't enough) is a pie "hitting the lens" of the camera. The audience, therefore, receive the final invective thrust.

The two-reel comedies, a very important part of the comedy spectrum of the period, were considered by the audience to be a vital part of the total programme at the movie theatre. Vitaphone, in an advertisement plugging its products, pushed the idea that a person shouldn't miss "half the fun" by stretching the point too far. "The feature picture is only about one-half the show," declared Vitaphone in stressing the entertainment value of Vitaphone Varieties' one- and two-reel creations. In 1930 they listed jazz music by Horace Heidt, opera by Martinelli, and the work of many comedians—among those listed were Fred Allen and Bert Lahr. Quite often these shorts were low budget productions with bad writing and directing. Early in the Thirties they were often mere recordings of the "turns" that had been created for the vaudeville stage. By 1931 there appeared more works written especially for the movies. After various attempts to be feature comedians, Buster Keaton and Harry Langdon retired to the production of two-reel pictures. Since they were both excellent gag men, a few of their works still hold up today. Produced for Educational Studios, Keaton's *Gold Ghost* (1935) and *Grand Slam Opera* (1936) boasted talents in gag writing and acting seldom shown by other comedians in shorts. *Knight Duty* (1933), starring Harry Langdon, contained some excellent gags and indicated that his acting skills were still in top form. By the late Thirties both actors moved to Columbia, and the quality of their films declined.

Actors who were beginning their careers also made shorts. Success, of sorts, in two-reelers often led to roles in features and, if the actor caught the fancy of the public, he might eventually become a leading player and a star. Today we can list some examples of the leading actors and actresses in two-reelers: Benny Rubin, *The Messenger Boy* (1931); Jack Benny, *Taxi Tangle* (1931), Bing Crosby, *Sing, Bing, Sing* (1931); Patsy Kelly and Thelma Todd, *Air Freight* (1933); Ben Blue, *All Sealed Up* (1934); Betty Grable, *A Quiet Fourth* (1935); and Bob Hope, *Shop Talk* (1935). For the most part, these two-reelers, viewed from today's perspective, are inferior works that reflect the limited abilities of comedians in a training period. Some would eventually become feature stars in a matter of a few years. Some would remain as bit or supporting actors throughout the Thirties.

While an Academy Award for Laurel and Hardy's talents in *The Music Box* (1932) seems justified, a similar award for *Bored of Education* (1936) starring the Our Gang kids might be questioned. This sentimental, light comedy probably touched the hearts of everyone in the industry because Our Gang represented a contribution to the Americana of the times. The series had been operating since 1922 with a variety of child actors. The gags in *Bored of Education* are simple and promote a few chuckles. Although the film was directed to the young moviegoer, many adults found it enjoyable and nostalgic. Problems of small fry fascinated the public, and the series continued to be produced by the Roach studio into the late Thirties. A feature length film, *General Spanky,* was created in 1936 by Roach but evidently didn't have a successful enough format to continue. Roach continued with two-reelers for two more years. "Our Gang" was then sold to M-G-M, which discontinued the series in 1944, making the total run of this type of comedy twenty-two years. Television obtained some of Roach's films in the Fifties, and kid comedies of the Thirties once more became popular. Only one of the Our Gang actors became successful in features. Jackie Cooper appeared in effective films like *Skippy* (1931), *The Champ* (1931), *Treasure Island* (1934), and *Peck's Bad Boy* (1934). Members of Our Gang who are best remembered are three boys, George "Spanky" MacFarland, Carl "Alfalfa" Switzer, and Billy "Buckwheat" Thomas —child actors who were teamed together in the mid-Thirties.

The full gamut of comedy by minor comedians would not be complete without a recognition of those excellent bit and supporting actors who fleshed out several comedies in the period. Some have already been mentioned because of their contributions to the works of major comedians. One minor comedian with many roles to his credit, most of them bit parts, is the delightful Franklin Pangborn. One of his best roles was that of J. Pinkerton Snoopington in W. C. Fields's *The Bank Dick* (1940), but he appeared in about seventy movies during the Thirties. Assisting Fields as a comic heavy in the 1940 *My Little Chickadee* was Margaret Hamilton as Mrs. Gideon. The supporting role of The Witch in the *Wizard of Oz* (1939) can be considered to be her strongest contribution. She had roles in over thirty movies during the period.

It would be difficult to discuss the contributions of so many others. The list is very long, but a few who come to mind as comedians who helped make the depression years brighter are Donald Meek, Frank McHugh, Hugh Herbert, Zasu Pitts, Alison Skipworth, Eugene Pallette, Sig Rumann, Guy Kibbee, Edward Everett Horton, Joan Davis, Andy Devine, and William Frawley. Others left out of this listing became more prominent in the Forties, and everyone listed continued into the Forties and later. Some were more popular—Joan Davis, for example, had leading roles in the Forties; Andy Devine got parts with more meat, playing many comic "side-kicks" to the leading man.

Where are comedian-character actors in the movies today? Few of the old timers are left, and there doesn't seem to be much chance for development of a new crop of talented bit and supporting actors of the same calibre as those of the Thirties.

VITAPHONE

JOINS TWO JOYOUS STARS IN ONE GREAT COMEDY SPECIAL

Funniest thing on four feet—Joe E. Brown and Winnie Lightner . . .

Teaming for the first time, in a picture teeming with laughs!

"HOLD EVERYTHING" held all hilarity records in its one-year run on Broadway . . .

Now here it is on the talking screen, with every riotous roar retained by *Vitaphone*.

"'Hold Everything' is a riot . . . rich and rare" . . . "full of the best 'gags' ever developed"—say famous newspaper experts who have seen it.

But don't take their word for it.— See for yourself!

Use the Vitaphone sign as a guide to the best of good times. It appears only on pictures produced by Warner Bros. and First National Pictures. "Vitaphone" is the registered trademark of The Vitaphone Corporation.

WARNER BROS. present

HOLD EVERYTHING

ALL IN TECHNICOLOR *with*
JOE E. BROWN ★ WINNIE LIGHTNER
Georges Carpentier ★ Sally O'Neil ★ Dorothy Revier
Abe Lyman and His Band

Warner Brothers' 1930 ad for Joe E. Brown's first starring film.

Song of the West (1930) shows Brown as the butt of
a practical joke.

In one of three baseball comedies, *Alibi Ike* (1935),
with Roscoe Karns (centre).

To the sceptical girl back home, Carol Hughes, he demonstrates a toy he wants to sell in *Earthworm Tractors* (1936).

In *Polo Joe* (1936) producing his famous comic yell.

As Osgood Fielding III, one of his last roles in *Some Like It Hot* (1959).

Leon Errol with Stuart Erwin in *Only Saps Work* (1930).

Patsy Kelly pays more attention to a friend (Guinn "Big Boy" Williams) than her job in *Kelly the Second* (1936) as her boss (Charlie Chase) looks on.

A 1937 publicity still of Edgar Kennedy showing his distinctive slow burn reaction to a faulty drinking fountain.

A still of Billy Gilbert showing him engaged in one of his many professional type comic roles.

A characteristic pose of Arthur Lake as the frustrated
Dagwood Bumstead of the "Blondie" series.

Lahr with Hugh Cameron and Ethel Merman in the 1939 theatre piece, *Du Barry Was a Lady*.

A stage production, *The Show Is On* in 1936, with Bert Lahr doing the "Song of the Woodchopper," influenced the comedian's motion picture acting.

Jimmy Durante with Shirley Temple in *Little Miss Broadway* (1938).

Vaudeville team Bobby Clark and Paul McCullough
created many two-reel films for Fox and RKO.

Old-timers Joe Weber and Lew Fields had a brief
revival on radio but had little success in the movies.

Silent screen star Ben Turpin appeared occasionally in bit parts such as the role of an incompetent handyman (with Oliver Hardy) in *Saps at Sea* (1940).

As chief of police Ford Sterling (centre) directs his bungling crew in the two reel 1935 curiosity, *Keystone Hotel.*

Don't miss 1/

VITAPHONE VARIETIES ARE HALF THE FUN

OF ANY EVENING AT THE THEATRE

/2 the fun!

Look for these New Headliners—

Vitaphone Varieties will introduce you to Ann Pennington, Irene Franklin, Fred Allen, Bert Lahr, Eddie Buzzell, Jack Buchanan, Miller & Lyles, and scores of others, in the "specialties" that have made them Broadway sensations.

And Clever Novelties—

Fred Keating, whose feats of comedy magic are now the talk of New York — Little Billy, the world's most celebrated midget — Bobby Gillette and his two-man banjo—and Eddie Lambert, amazing trick pianist.

The Best in Every Field—

Look forward to jazz by Horace Heidt; opera by Martinelli and Charles Hackett; comedy by vaudeville headliners; and short-story sketches with Blanche Sweet, William Boyd, etc.

"Vitaphone" is the registered trademark of The Vitaphone Corporation. Color Scenes are by the Technicolor Process.

YOU'RE entitled to two hours of entertainment at your talking picture theatre. The feature picture is only about one-half the show . . . The rest is made up of one- and two-reel featurettes.

Unless THE WHOLE SHOW *is good, you get only* HALF THE FUN *you paid for!*

• • •

Now for the first time there is a way to insure full value for your entertainment money—make sure that the short pictures on the bill are VITAPHONE VARIETIES. VITAPHONE VARIETIES is the group name chosen to designate an entirely new type of short screen subjects. With this vastly improved series of miniature screen masterpieces, Warner Bros. bring to short features for the first time all the class and

dignity of the finest full-length productions.

In VITAPHONE VARIETIES, slapstick is superseded by renowned stars and acts in specialties that have made them outstanding attractions in famous Broadway shows....

VITAPHONE VARIETIES are the first short pictures to introduce original songs written specially for them by popular composers . . .

And VITAPHONE VARIETIES will present the first series of tabloid musical comedies ever filmed in Full Natural Color !

• • •

Don't miss half the fun . . . Don't hesitate to ask your theatre manager to show VITAPHONE VARIETIES every week . . . He will be glad to know your preference so that he can more closely accomodate your tastes.

SOMETHING <u>NEW</u> IN TABLOID TALKING PICTURES

VITAPHONE VARIETIES
Insure Full Value for your Entertainment Money

The Vitaphone branch of Warner Brothers in 1930 plugged its short subjects as "half the fun" and "half the show."

Our Gang (*circa* 1935) with the best known kids, George "Spanky" MacFarland and Billy "Buckwheat" Thomas (left) and Carl "Alfalfa" Switzer with the sandwich (right).

Franklin Pangborn as J. Pinkerton Snoopington in *The Bank Dick* (1940) with W. C. Fields.

Margaret Hamilton as Mrs. Gideon in *My Little Chicka-adee* (1940).

The witch in *The Wizard of Oz* (1939) proved to be
Miss Hamilton's most famous role.

In *Gold Diggers of 1935* Hugh Herbert had the lion's
share of the comedy scenes.

Edward Everett Horton in trouble, *Oh Doctor!* (1937).

7

Sophisticated and Almost Satirical

Although sophisticated comedy had existed on the stage since the Sixteenth century, the formative age of cinema produced few examples of the mode. Since this kind of drama's strongest quality was its wit—the clever line of dialogue, it developed as a major *genre* only with the coming of sound. From critics in the Thirties it received the labels "screwball," "daffy," and "madcap" comedy. This type of film enjoyed its greatest vogue between 1934 and 1938. In the early Forties it was revived through the talented direction and writing of Preston Sturges.

Some of the memorable movies of the Thirties appeared in 1937. Among the best serious and humorous films of the year were *Lost Horizon, Camille, A Star Is Born, Dead End, You Only Live Once, The Road Back, The Good Earth, The Life of Emile Zola, Easy Living, Nothing Sacred,* and *Topper.* Credit for such a fruitful year may be given to the outstanding direction of Leo Mc-Carey, Frank Capra, George Stevens, William Wellman, Fritz Lang, Victor Fleming, and James Whale. Of equal importance to the public who loved comedy were the fine humorous writers, Preston Sturges, Ben Hecht, and Bella and Samuel Spewack, plus the stars Carole Lombard, Irene Dunne, Cary Grant, and Fredric March who were engaged in the creation of sophisticated comedy.

In 1939 a portion of the last chapter of Lewis Jacobs's *Rise of the American Film* shows considerable insight into this field even though the evaluator was so close in time to his subject:

> The loss of credibility in former values, the breakdown of the smugness and self-confidence of the jazz era, the growing bewilderment and dissatisfaction in a "crazy" world that does not make sense, has been reflected in the revival of comedies of satire and self-ridicule . . .

These films were all sophisticated, mature, full of violence—hitting, falling, throwing, acrobatics—bright dialogue, slapstick action—all imbued with terrific energy.

Since the films with these characteristics are light and gay in tone, Jacobs may be inaccurate when he labels this madcap comedy "satire." Nevertheless, there was a brush with important social and psychological values that made this mode the most interesting in the gamut of comedy in the Thirties.

Two movies, *Easy Living* and *Nothing Sacred,* created in 1937, illustrate the many characteristics of the madcap comedy film which evolved from the high society comedy of the stage. The metamorphosis of the sophisticated comedy developed when screenwriters and film directors began to employ romantic situations and slapstick comedy that were particular to the screen medium.

While no prototype of screwball comedy can be said to contain the essence of the *genre, Easy Living* has the facets necessary for it to serve as a model. A lampoon of the Cinderella story, the movie shows the intricate involvements of the life of a penniless young girl named Mary Smith (Jean Arthur) with millionaire banker J. B. Ball (Edward Arnold) and his son (Ray Milland). To spite his wife's extravagance in clothes, J. B. Ball takes the zany action of a screwball comedy character and throws her expensive sable coat from the top of a building. Riding on the top deck of a bus in the street below J. B.'s expensive apartment, Mary Smith finds that the coat has landed in her lap. From such a wild coincidence an elaborate, farcical plot full of many intrigues develops. Trying to return the coat to magnate Ball, she receives from him not only the coat but a new hat as well. Since the purchase is made in the dress and hat shop of gossipy Van Buren

(Franklin Pangborn), hotel owner Louis Louis (Luis Alberni) receives the news and believes an illicit relationship exists between Mary Smith and J. B. Realising that J. B. Ball will soon become the receiver of his hotel for lack of payments on a loan, Louis contacts Mary and arranges for her to live in the Imperial suite of his hotel. The accommodations fit the label—the suite has a series of rooms fit for a king and queen. Believing her good fortune to be part of an elaborate publicity scheme, Mary moves to the pinnacle of the affluent life. Merchants receive the rumour as an opportunity to influence J. B. Ball through his mistress, and a deluge of expensive gifts arrive each day at the hotel suite. But as such farce dramas operate, Mary meets J. B.'s son, and an affair develops without the identification of all parties concerned being revealed until the resolution of the story. To complicate the farce even more, J. B.'s wife goes to Florida, and the husband stays in the same hotel as Mary.

The most unique comedy idea develops from the reactions of the people who observe the alleged affair. The hotel owner, called Louie by everyone, gives *carte blanche* use of his facilities to Mary. Van Buren sends his clothes to be modelled to promote his concern. Soon the whole business world showers gifts on the supposed mistress of the famous "Bull of Broadstreet." Finally, all fashionable people decide to move to the Hotel Louie because they wish to be associated with high society and the "swinging set"—as the modern vernacular might classify this situation.

Two areas bordering on satire are in operation in *Easy Living*. The frantic exploitation of the business world is lampooned and the "upper crust" is seen as those who have inverted values when it comes to ideas on love and marriage. Unfortunately, this film drama by Preston Sturges does not fully exploit all the possibilities of the humour. There is not the sting of satire—the invective that exposes completely such folly. Nevertheless, the satirical lines of comedy are strong enough to approach a solid lampoon or burlesque of high society.

Of even greater significance to the fabrication of sophisticated-madcap comedy is the use of licence. While many humorous dramas have a degree of licence, the screwball mode explodes with this quality of freedom. The heroes and heroines often do almost anything they wish. Even minor situations allow the individual to engage in a caprice shunned by respectable and proper people in the society. *Easy Living* is replete with moments in which the individual "does his thing" or takes action that might be considered illogical behaviour. Even though J. B. Ball pinches pennies in his household, he gets great delight in grabbing and throwing away his wife's $10,000 sable coat just to show her who is the boss. Later J. B.'s cook engages in a favourite day dream—he tells his employer off. Smouldering from the insult his professional pride ordering him to use lard instead of butter, the cook raves: "Go fry yourself in lard, you dirty capitalist!" J. B. retaliates physically by breaking a bowl over the cook's head; the assault gives great pleasure to the tycoon, and he laughs gleefully. On a lighter level is Mary's impulsive purchase of two sheep dogs and two parrots that cause problems for everyone else in the Louie Hotel and Ball's office.

On a slapstick level the licence of robbing a food automat can be observed in a scene in which the tripping of a lever that opens all the dispensing windows brings a horde to the establishment. People, many of them panhandlers, stream into the automat to grab the exposed food. Because no one seems satisfied with just one tray of food, comic fights develop as this crush of humanity wallows in an orgy of gluttony. Such bizarre scenes were one of the staples of the sophisticated-madcap comedy.

Because the tone of this type of comedy was very light, a more subterranean level of licence developed. The role of women was revealed in a new light in an age that hadn't heard of the severe demands of a women's liberation movement. The comic heroine usually was allowed the same liberties as the male in the sophisticated film comedy of the Thirties. She may have been very playful and charming, but she did what she wanted to do. Often her action was muted by a genuine innocence, but she ended up with the man in a bed. In *Easy Living* Mary lives with J. B. Jr. in the Imperial suite. She also is capable of leading any male into a desire to "live it up"—to buy something or just have fun without a thought about tomorrow.

Easy Living, like many comedies of its kind, does not have the witty dialogue that is particularly noteworthy out of context. The dialogue is often functional; it matches the given situation. Broad comedy characters like that played by Luis Alberni often have the most quotable lines, but lines that also suffer when removed from their context. His fractured English operates in a fashion similar to

Chico Marx's. To his high society guests Louie reveals his weird choice of words when he refers to his plush hotel: "What a place to flop!" And also, "What kind of a dump do you think this is?" When he doesn't want to get involved, Louie declares, "I don't want to be complicated."

Easy Living contains many intrigues that need not be cited. It is only necessary to conclude this examination by indicating that the film combines all the elements of the high comedy stage play with the romantic and slapstick comedy traditions of cinema. The emphasis on licence that has been a technique not fully explored by critics creates a change in the overall tone of the romantic or boy meets girl theme. A look at *Nothing Sacred* will clarify the uniqueness of the treatment of this theme.

The production *Nothing Sacred* had the fortune of a good script by Ben Hecht, clean-cut directing by William A. Wellman, and two formidable stars, Carole Lombard and Fredric March, plus two first-rate supporting character actors, Charles Winninger and Walter Connolly. The attack on society was direct. To show the direction in which he levelled his guns, Hecht used the following opening statement in three titles, with a series of shots of statues and buildings and a view of Times Square:

Title #1 This is New York
          Skyscraper Champion
          of the World . . .
Title #2 Where the Slickers and
          Know-It-Alls peddle gold
          bricks to each other . . .
Title #3 . . . And where Truth,
          Crushed to earth, rises
          again more phony
          than a glass eye . . .

In 1934 Hecht, with the assistance of Charles McArthur, adapted a stage play, *Napoleon of Broadway*, to the screen under the title of *Twentieth Century*. It attempts to expose the phoniness of artists in the theatre—especially directors and actors. Its successor, *Nothing Sacred*, uses a similar light treatment, and neither work amounts to stinging satire. But the comic attack, while awkwardly and crudely stated in the opening title of *Nothing Sacred*, has more sting than most of the lampoons that can be termed madcap comedies. Hecht's target in *Nothing Sacred* is all people in society who wallow in bathos for the plight of an individual about to die. He attacks the sob sister social manifestation with his pen dipped in quinine wa-

ter rather than acid. Nevertheless, the results are delightful and, at times, hit home effectively.

Every principal character, interestingly enough, is engaged in bilking someone else in this comic drama. The hero, who might be more aptly called the anti-hero, Wally Cook (Fredric March) desires to get back in the good graces of his editor, Oliver Stone (Walter Connolly) by developing and exploiting a small town New England girl named Hazel Flagg (Carole Lombard) who has been reported to be dying of radium poisoning. Even though Hazel learns from her alcoholic physician (Charles Winninger) that the latest test proves she has no illness, she desires to see New York. When Wally, thinking she is still ill, offers to take her to the big city in order to write stories on her plight, Hazel and her doctor take advantage of the situation—the exploiters are exploited by their victims.

As in *Easy Living*, Hazel, like Mary, is wined and dined in a palatial hotel. Furthermore, Hazel receives the key to the city, is saluted at a night club as the heroine of the age, and becomes the subject of the leading feature story for the *Morning Star* through Wally Cook's articles. With some awkwardness that soon vanishes Hazel Flagg enjoys the attention and adoration that she receives from the public. Eventually she is exposed, but she remains formidable enough to keep the deception going for some time. She and Wally fall in love, but as in many of the madcap comedies of the times, there is only a pinch of sentiment. The woman exercises as much, if not more, of her will in the affair as the man does. *Nothing Sacred* does not have a moment that would appeal to the sentimentalist; the relationship between the man and the woman, even though it may verge on the genteel emotion, eventually and directly undercuts the type of drama that would provoke a tear.

A series of jabs at society and the individual emerges both in the plotting and in the dialogue of *Nothing Sacred*. A good but hardly original sequence develops when Wally Cook finds himself pitted against the stoic New England temperament as he receives only "Yeps" and "Nopes" from a railroad station manager. "What's your name— Coolidge?" Wally asks. With the rancour of the small-town dipsomaniac, Dr. Downer abuses the profession of journalism by ranting, "The Lord God reaching down into the mire couldn't elevate one of them to the depth of degradation." Wally receives non-verbal attacks from old ladies who glare at him and young boys who pelt him with fruit from a passing wagon. His final humiliation takes place when a toddler runs from behind a gate and bites him on the leg.

What historian-critic Lewis Jacobs calls "bright dialogue" assists in the creation of humour in *Nothing Sacred* and proves to be much stronger than the lines from *Easy Living*. Of his editor's disposition, for example, Wally observes, "He's got a different quality of charm. He's sort of a cross between a ferris wheel and a werewolf—but with a lovable streak, if you care to blast for it." From the small-town Hazel unconscious dark humour develops as she bubbles gayly with anticipation of her high life in New York: "I'm not going to go to bed until I have convulsions and my teeth start falling out." Later when she is "doing the town" with Wally, she shows a practical streak as the reporter observes people moping and shedding tears for her:

WALLY: (*Disgustedly*) For good clean fun there's nothing like a wake.
HAZEL: Oh, please, please, let's not talk shop.

Eventually, Wally cannot resist her charms, even when she is supposed to be under a sentence of death. He asks for her hand in marriage. "But, darling," she points out, "there's no future in it."

While written, verbal comedy for the screen seemed to have disappeared with the silent film, it is evident in *Nothing Sacred*. Hazel composes two letters which appear on the front page of the "Morning Star." When she decides to feign suicide (Dr. Downer promises to fish her from the water), she writes:

Dear New York City,
Goodbye. Remember me as someone you made very happy. I enjoyed everything. There is only one thing left to enjoy—your river . . .

A beautiful girl, as all who saw her picture in the paper know, Hazel pens this note as she is forced to leave to avoid a city wide exposure of her deception:

Dear New York City,
We've had a lot of good times together, you and I. But even the best of times must end so I've gone to face the end alone like an elephant.

Several situations of a physical and wacky nature in *Nothing Sacred* are necessary ingredients for this type of comedy film. Hazel's phony suicide turns into an unsuccessful ruse when Wally races to the rescue. He lunges to grab her as she stands posed to jump off a wharf; he stumbles and falls against her so that both plunge into the river. He can't swim, naturally, and Hazel rescues him. In another scene of physical action Wally comes to Hazel's aid when her deception is about to be exposed. He engages in an elaborate mock fist fight to make her weak enough to flunk a physical examination. For a finish to this fight, Wally intentionally knocks her unconscious with a sharp jab to the jaw. When she awakes, she finds that the editor of the "Morning Star" has observed the fight behind the screen, and her feigned illness has been revealed. Angry with Wally's fight scheme and smarting from an aching jaw, she socks Wally on the chin and knocks him unconscious. Similar physical battles between the sexes were often incorporated in the screwball comedy. This type of action helped to give the mode its label.

At the fade-out Wally and Hazel are on their honeymoon, incognito. They have not repented and are obviously enjoying a "what-the-hell" attitude toward the society that has engaged in the folly of sentimentality. This last touch may be objectionable to some evaluators of the movie, but I find it an excellent stroke of characterisation that reinforces the attempt at social satire. Too many of the sophisticated comedies of the Forties and quite a few in the Thirties tended to compromise the ending of the sentimental drama by having a reformation of sorts in the mating of the romantic leads. At its zenith of quality the screwball, madcap, or daffy film comedy avoided the sentimental ending.

One of the dramas that provided the roots for the development of the sophisticated comedy suffered the weakness of the sentimental ending. The 1931 *Bachelor Apartment*, starring Lowell Sherman, Irene Dunne, and Mae Murray, had all the ingredients of a sophisticated film comedy, but it lacked the slapstick scenes to place it in the classification of screwball comedy. A worldly, hedonistic attitude toward sex and a series of bedroom intrigues during a good portion of the film produced effective anti-sentimental humour. A wealthy rake, Wayne Carter, gets into many amusing scrapes because he has designs on almost every female he meets. He even goes to the point of taking his chauffeured limousine to the streets to hunt for more "game." While the comedy incorporates many women who are gold diggers and who will do anything for the high life, Elaine Andrews (Irene Dunne) is the long-suffering, older sister who admits that she wouldn't mind having a wealthy man, but she will get him the proper way—by marrying him. Sentiment and conventional morality creep in through Elaine's stand and mute the sharpness of a comedy that began with satirical promise. Eventually, the rake is reformed in much the same manner as that of the sentimental British comedy of the early Eighteenth century—a distinct dramatic degeneration from the more laughable, witty works of the Restoration theatre.

The strongest breakthrough for sophisticated sexual comedy was made by Mae West. The unabashed woman who takes pleasure in her sexuality and ability to control men with her physical charms was delectably burlesqued in her 1933 works *She Done Him Wrong* and *I'm No Angel*. In these movies she played the gaudy, kept woman who enjoyed her position in society, the comforts and the influence obtained by successful women in her trade. Derived from the stage play, *Diamond Lil,* which Miss West wrote for herself in 1929, *She Done Him Wrong* was the weaker of the two films. Nevertheless, the movie had much to recommend it. Mae's dialogue was sprinkled with *double entendres,* usually linked with sex. When asked if she'd ever met a man who could make her happy, she replied with her famous drawl, a clenched jaw, and a smile: "Sure. Lots of times." And there were the now well-known Mae's maxims such as, "When women go wrong, men go right after them." As in some of her later films, the total work did not have a strong comic design. An old-fashioned, serious love triangle held the story together. Sprinkled into the melodrama, two songs, "I Wonder Where My Easy Rider's Gone" and "I Like a Man Who Takes His Time," gave Mae a chance to make further sexual comments and displayed her talents with the torch song and the blues. The titles of the songs, of course, employ double meanings.

I'm No Angel, released during the latter part of 1933, displayed not only a definite improvement over the *Diamond Lil* adaptation; it was Mae West's most distinguished contribution to the sophisticated comedy film. Her link with the underworld in *I'm No Angel* was rather melodramatic, but her bed hopping in high society created a comic framework for the total work. The haughtiness of her characterisation of Tira, a carnival dancer, was an upswing from her portrayal of Lou in *She Done Him Wrong.* Tira often engaged in the put-down with the relish, if not the zip, of a Groucho Marx. When her boss, played

by the daddy of all big deals, Edward Arnold, made a conciliatory gesture by stating, "Tira, I've changed my mind." "Yeah," she cracked, "Does it work any better?" With the aggression of Alexander the Great, Tira took over her own defence in a trial, charming the judge and jury with her asides, wisecracks, and put-downs. In this film some of the famous Mae West lines were used. After a verbal fight with a woman she drawled to her servant: "Beulah, peel me a grape." To a man, fluttering her eye lashes, she observed, "When I'm good, I'm very good, but when I'm bad *(very long pause),* I'm better." As a gilded, tainted sage she uttered, "It's not the men in your life that counts —it's the life in your men." Most remembered and most often repeated (with variations) was the line: "And don't forget—come up and see me sometime."

Miss West's humour was not merely verbal. It consisted of a provocative walk, a toss of the head or hip, or a glint in the eye. She was a personality comedienne with a particular style of her own. Actually, she never possessed thespian skills with dimension. There was a monotony in her delivery and amazingly few acting tricks up her sleeve. This slender talent with an ample body made her a legend in her time and very camp in the Sixties.

While *I'm No Angel* might be said to be her best and most typical work, she was teamed with naïve, rough but lovable Victor McLaglen in a feature that probably helped to produce her most effective acting job. The work, *Klondike Annie* (1936) had a story line that forced her into a change of identity. To escape the law she assumes the role of a woman religious leader in a ministry that has been losing ground because the evils of a booming, bawdy frontier community are too much for the average person bent on taming and reforming an environment so loaded with sin. Annie's tainted background, of course, has taught her to deal with seemingly untameable men, and she has the necessary hucksterism to sell religion in the wilds of Alaska. Since Miss West's sexual wit had nearly been eliminated by the Hays Office, Annie was a mild version of her Lou and Tira. Despite the handicap Mae was an effective actress in this film, and it proved that if she had the right script and a male lead like McLaglen, she could still produce good pictures. Annie's employment of high handed tactics to "win souls" may remind present day audiences of some of the methods used by religious leaders in today's society.

In 1934 three films, *Twentieth Century, It*

Happened One Night, and *The Thin Man,* illustrated the evolution of the sophisticated comedy as it moved closer to its zenith.

If *Twentieth Century* had no other virtue, the recording of the comic acting skills of one of the outstanding actors of stage and screen, John Barrymore, would suffice to make the film a hallmark in cinema history. However, the total film is a superior example of sophisticated comedy. Carole Lombard, cast opposite John Barrymore, proved herself a formidable comedienne. The comic idea dealt with a squabble between two egos, male and female, and was more than a battle of the sexes—it was a war between two creative people.

As I observed earlier, the woman in the sophisticated comedy had achieved a status nearly equal to that of the male. Part of this manifestation may have resulted from the functional aspect. That is, a way to achieve comedy in a male dominated society was to place the female on an equal plane or higher in order to create the necessary—and humorous—inversion of status. The comic drama has used this device since ancient time. In 411 B.C. Aristophanes's *Lysistrata* had the women of Athens and all important city states of Greece staging a sex strike to force their war loving husbands to declare peace. Sexual humour can be cited as the essential part of the total work, but the inversion of status, the women taking over to the humiliation of the men, becomes the focus of the satire.

Twentieth Century does not have women or a woman taking over, but a stage and screen star, Lily Garland (Carole Lombard), makes the impressario-director Oscar Jeffe (John Barrymore) grovel. Like a modern day David Belasco Jeffe moulds Lily into a great actress, but the mentor becomes an unbearable tyrant to her and she rebels. The evolving nature of the screwball comedy becomes evident in the hard-fought verbal confrontations which occasionally degenerate into humorous physical fights, similar to but not as elaborate as that type of action employed in *Nothing Sacred.* Another feature of the daffy sophisticated comedy was the use of eccentrics. *Twentieth Century* has a religious fanatic called Mr. Clark (Etienne Girardot), who sneakily pastes "Repent" stickers on windows and lampshades of the club car of the train plus the hats and coats of people as they pass by the weird little man. This harmless odd ball gets caught several times and pathetically admits that his obsession has disturbed the passengers on the train, the Twentieth Century. He promises never to bother anyone again, and

his stickers are taken away from him. However, his one-track mind cannot be halted; he rescues his stickers from the waste basket and starts pasting furiously again. This little man's wacky activities become a running gag, but he also becomes an integral part of the plot when he writes a bogus check to back Jeffe's wild plan to produce the Passion play featuring Lily as Mary Magdalene.

Some of the cleverest comedy of the film derives from the character of Oscar Jeffe, the epitome of the egotist who tries to manipulate everyone with his flowery, emotion charged speeches. He uses self-pity, bathos, heroics, and artistic pretentiousness. His stock opening oration to the cast of a play he is staging is loaded with false flattery:

> Now, before we begin, I want you all to remember one thing: No matter what I may say, no matter what I may do on this stage during our work *(pauses and shifts to tender tones)*—I love you all . . . Above everything in the world I love the theatre and the charming people in it.

His hypocrisy in this statement is exposed when he is forced to act the role of an old-fashioned southern gentleman to escape the law. He confides to his manager, "I never thought I should sink so low as to become an actor." His deceptiveness also becomes comic when he tries to bargain with Lily. He has had an affair with her and now has to approach the star when she is with her present *amour.* Hastily improvising an arm sling to avoid a physical attack, he explains magnanimously:

> OSCAR: I came here out of a gallant mood—I congratulate you.
> GEORGE: And you can get right out again! You've no right here.
> OSCAR: No right? Doesn't he know about us? *(With an affected, dramatic tone)* I thought everybody knew. It was one of the great romances of our time.
> GEORGE: You! *(He threatens—about to strike him.)*
> OSCAR: *(Pointing to his arm.)* I broke it in Chicago.

But Lily can usually see through his histrionics. When he threatens suicide by cutting his throat if she does not come back to him, she cracks, "If you did, grease paint would run out of it."

Most significant of all in this relationship between man and woman in *Twentieth Century* is the obviousness of the game that is played. Almost all emotions are feigned or at least exaggerated to obtain a reaction from the other party. There is no room in these celebrities' lives for the sentiments of the average lovers. A worldly-wise game of love in which the most clever manipulator wins, regardless of the deception, links the drama to English Restoration. In fact, that person who wins is supposed to be admired as one possessing true wit. A different standard of morality or even what some would call amorality exists in the world of the sophisticated comedy.

In 1934 director Frank Capra and screenwright Robert Riskin concocted an earthier, warmer type of screwball comedy that indicated a direction which eventually led to a mixed *genre,* as unlikely as this may seem, using elements of both sophisticated and sentimental comedy. *It Happened One Night* has (as well as its share of clever dialogue) an urbane attitude toward sex. Thematically, the film comes closer to the sentimental comedy. Bosley Crowther, in *The Great Films: Fifty Golden Years of Motion Pictures,* detects the nature of this mixture and comments:

> The gist of this frisky recounting of a romance that burgeons between a millionaire's runaway daughter and a roguish newspaperman who are brought into unlikely contact on a bus trip from Miami to New York is that one doesn't need money to have a good time. Indeed, money and high social station are supreme disadvantages. And the blissful and buoyant realization the girl finally gets through her head is that these things can be well abandoned for the greater satisfactions of true love. Obviously such an outpouring of unrealistic romance would be and would have been bromidic, even to the audiences of its day, who were hardly empathetic to social snootiness and wealth, if it weren't done with enough versatility, ingenuity and quick colloquial wit to disguise its essential nonsense and its incongruities.

Later Frank Capra was to be known for his palatable sentimental works, *Mr. Deeds Goes to Town* (1936), *You Can't Take It with You* (1938), and *Mr. Smith Goes to Washington* (1939). The slickness of his directing—the light touch with each emotional scene and his ability to gain convincing, spontaneous performances from his actors—made it possible to sell sentiment and bromides to the populace. In *It Happened One Night* he fends off the underlying sentiment with touches of humour and keeps the action lively. When the couple are forced to share a room together, Ellie (Claudette Colbert) objects to the possible loss of her modesty and virtue. Peter (Clark Gable) places a blanket between their beds and declares: "Behold the walls of Jericho! Maybe not as thick as the ones Joshua blew down with his trumpet, but a lot safer." He does not have a trumpet, of course, and is a man

of honour. The fade-out of the film shows the "walls of Jericho" (the blanket) falling because they have been married.

A more worldly-wise and more sophisticated view of male and female was displayed in *The Thin Man* (1934), a film adapted from Dashiell Hammett's detective story. In this case the couple are married but exhibit the antithesis of the sedate role society has often assigned to the state of wedlock. Nick and Nora Charles tease each other about their relationship and their contact with others of the opposite sex. When Nick has been seen with a young girl, his wife chides him, but he uses the perfect put-down. Referring to the girl, he remarks, "Yes, very nice type." "You got types?" asks Nora sarcastically. "Only you, darling," drawls Nick. "Lanky brunettes with wicked jaws." Nonchalantly she expresses the view that if he goes to investigate a murder, he might be killed himself. "You wouldn't be a widow long . . ." Nora stabs with an interruption, "You bet I wouldn't!" Nick continues, ". . . not with all your money."

This suave view of their relationship extends to their party life. Nick lives with a drink in hand. When Nora meets her husband at a bar after Christmas shopping, she learns that he has already had five martinis and is on his sixth one. Not to be outdone she requests a line up of five drinks in a row so she can catch up with her husband. When Nick avoids details of his criminal investigation before the press, a frustrated reporter asks if there's anything he can tell about the case. "Yes," Nick shoots back, "It's putting me way behind in my drinking."

Sophisticated films of this type are clearly the antithesis of the family comedy. *The Thin Man* depicts the lovers of a fast life. Since danger is also Nick's hobby, he takes on another dimension. He is an amateur detective with more brains than the entire police force—a modern day, penthouse version of Sherlock Holmes. Nick even playfully refers to his side-kick wife, Nora, who helps him with his investigation, as "Watson." Furthermore, the wife has the wit of the put-down that matches his. When Nick Charles starts the long *dénouement* so typical of the detective story formula, he engages in a long monologue before the guests (most of whom are suspects in the case of murder) can receive the first course of the meal. Nora slaps him verbally with acid charm: "It's the best dinner I ever listened to."

Another movie wife in the sophisticated comedy who loved high living was Marian Kirby (Constance Bennett) in the fantasy, *Topper* (1937).

Marian liked to dally with other men. In the original novel by Thorne Smith this wife was more of a female rake. As an ectoplasmic creature who returned to the land of the living after a fatal car accident, she would get between the sheets with a man. In the screen version she is merely a tease. Even so, she has a gaiety in her female rakishness that makes the screen characterisation a sharp lampoon of the fidelity usually expected of a wife. Sophisticated comedy, even in 1937, was clearly flaunting the absurdity of the rigid, double standard.

Actually, the rakishness of Marian Kirby in *Topper* is well-intentioned since she seeks the reform of Cosmos Topper, a wealthy banker who has become a drudge—a slave of his routine profession and the role he must play in a stuffy society. Throughout the work the comic idea operates on the concept of licence. The theme which was popular in the Thirties, expressed the idea that "you can't take it with you"—so live life to its fullest without the confines of duty. Work, which was not easy to find in those depression days anyway, was not the great virtue that puritan ethics had dictated to the populace. Comedy, in short, advocated a philosophy of "do your own thing" in that age.

The main story line of this fantasy concerns the efforts of two high life advocates, George and Marian Kirby, to do a good deed for a casual friend, Cosmos Topper. They make this decision when they realise they have been killed in a car accident and must remain on earth as ghosts until they earn the reward of the hereafter. Topper acknowledges his plight—the dreary, routine nature of his life—and becomes an easy prey for the "swinging" couple's plan to reform him. Much of the comedy is derived from Topper's awkward attempts to become a man of the world. Also, humour evolves from the ability of the Kirbys (played by Cary Grant and Constance Bennett) to play tricks on the world of the living. Marian Kirby can appear and disappear at will, much to the dismay of the house detective and the hotel manager, who have difficulty arresting Cosmos Topper for keeping a woman in his room.

The best verbal sophisticated humour involves the type of understatement found in British comedy and combines it with a frustrating situation. Topper, for example, becomes very agitated when he first meets the ectoplasmic Kirbys. In a discussion with them he resolves, "I refuse to say another word. I'm probably talking to myself anyway."

Some of the "lower class" character comedy comes from a bell-boy played by Arthur Lake and a house detective enacted by Eugene Pallette. Lake does an excellent job of expressing comic frustration when the erratic Kirbys appear and disappear as the bellboy tries his best to carry out his duties. Pallette also wrings humour from a display of frustration. A truth-revealing garble of words by the house detective when a company of policemen try to catch the ghosts makes the frustration even funnier: "A fine bunch of cops you are. I had that guy right where he wanted me until you crossed him up."

Another fantasy-sophisticated film comedy was scripted by the famous stage playwright, Robert Sherwood, and directed by one of France's leading cinema directors, René Clair. This work, *The Ghost Goes West* (1936), was produced by Alexander Korda and featured a British-American cast—Robert Donat, Jean Parker, Eugene Pallette, and Elsa Lanchester. As in *Topper,* humour was created in this work by the ghost who produced confusion, frustration, and fear when it was loose in the land of the living. Because the film integrated comedy into the fantasy, the labels often given to sophisticated comedy of the time, "zany," "wild," and "lunatic," might be applied to it. Some sentimental elements filtered in and cut the sharpness of the satire directed at the American *nouveau riche*. A crass, naïve business man, acted by Eugene Pallette, wants a castle for a private mansion and brings a Scottish castle, stone by stone, to the United States, to be re-constructed in a most unsuitable location, Florida. With the castle he gets a ghost. The rakish quality of the ghost (Robert Donat) in his desire for any woman has a sophisticated comedy bent, but when he latches on to a favourite girl, Peggy Martin (Jean Parker), the full potential of the humour begins to ebb into a sentimental romance. More noted for his serious plays, Robert Sherwood illustrated that he did not have the touch of the humorous writer. His scenario did not exploit or sustain all the comic possibilities.

Sentimental leanings tended to blunt the comedy of *Vivacious Lady* (1938), starring James Stewart and Ginger Rogers. This film remains as an example of a rather routine screwball comedy that features a college biology professor marrying a singer-dancer. The woman receives the label of a tainted woman in the educational community. The sexual wit, exploiting the difficulty of the husband in bedding his wife because he must keep the marriage a secret from his father, loses its edge because Stewart and Miss Rogers do not seem capable of broadening the acting to a comic level. Some scenes are funny, but the weak script cuts the effectiveness of the total work.

In *Mad Miss Manton* (1938) crime and comedy are combined in a manner similar to that used in *The Thin Man,* but the film has some difficulty getting off the ground with Barbara Stanwyck in the lead. With a weak script Henry Fonda, who proved himself an excellent low-keyed comedian in *The Lady Eve* (1941) and *The Male Animal* (1942), seems to be in the process of learning his trade.

Not fully recognised in its day was the 1937 production, *Woman Chases Man.* This work had the plot, characters, and effective acting to give it a high rating. For some unknown reason, screenwriters Samuel and Bella Spewack wrote the script and then wanted their names taken from the credits. New writers and directors entered the creative process, and it seemed that this work would be the dud that is often created from too much tampering with a drama. The heroine, played by Miriam Hopkins with considerable deftness, is an architect who ends up chasing rich, stuffy son who has taken over the management of his father's fortunes. The heroine, Virginia, has a great deal of difficulty getting her model suburban housing project accepted and finds it necessary to get the reserved young man drunk. When he becomes tipsy, he is as wild with the money as his father. A struggle to get the son to sign a contract for the project ends literally up a tree. Since the son is wild drunk, everyone must hazard a climb up the tree to get him to sign or prevent him from signing—almost parodying the exciting grapple for a pistol in a gangster or Western movie.

Two other films made in 1938, *Holiday* and *Bringing Up Baby,* may be cited to complete a study of the fascinating screwball comedy. *Holiday,* starring Katharine Hepburn, Cary Grant, Edward Everett Horton, and Lew Ayres, indicated a trend that would elevate the status of comedy. About

this time Katharine Hepburn's career was sagging; she was noted only for her serious roles in works like *Little Women.* Similarly engaged in playing serious roles, Irene Dunne demanded a comedy role and established herself as a very effective comedienne in director Leo McCarey's *The Awful Truth* (1937). *Holiday* the next year provided Miss Hepburn with a role in sophisticated comedy that would give her career a new dimension and establish the importance of the female star in such works. The film is a refurbished version of Philip Barry's 1928 stage play and concerns again the theme of freedom. A young man must choose between marrying an heiress and becoming rich or following his desire to stop money-grubbing and take a holiday. Miss Hepburn plays the part of a politically liberated young woman who is bent on reforming her tycoon father and, of course, she eventually wins the young man. While this role was one of her most outstanding jobs of acting, she appeared earlier in the year in *Bringing Up Baby*—a comedy that has more ingredients of the madcap film mode. Actor Cary Grant also appears opposite her in this picture. Under Howard Hawks's direction the film has the slapstick and chase elements plus the clever dialogue and characters that make the *genre* so lively and diverse in its humour.

The evolution and the fading of the sophisticated screwball comedy in the Thirties were linked to the tastes of the time and a tendency for Hollywood to repeat a good thing until successive works became poor imitations without the flair of the earlier models. A move to the sentimental, folksy drama may have been the strongest reason for the fading of this mode. In 1938 the family comedy was making its invasion, and the teenagers and moppets seemed to be in favour. It was an unfortunate take-over. The sophisticated madcap comedy never fully regained its footing even though it was destined to influence the entire gamut of comedy films that was produced in the Forties and Fifties.

—but they couldn't escape

"THIS THING CALLED LOVE"

with EDMUND LOWE
and CONSTANCE BENNETT

Ann and Robert weren't going to have the usual kind of marriage with its petty quarrels and hampering jealousies. So they tried a new plan—Ann drew a salary for her services as a homemaker— Bob could have all the girl friends he desired, she all the male admirers she wished. It worked fine until the green-eyed god elbowed his way in in spite of them! Rich in humor, full of clever dialog, penetrating in its satire on "modern marriage." THIS THING CALLED LOVE is grown-up entertainment, with a brilliant cast including Zasu Pitts, Carmelita Geraghty and Stuart Erwin.

ALL MUSIC—ALL SOUND—ALL DIALOGUE

Pathé Picture

DIRECTED BY PAUL STEIN   RALPH BLOCK PRODUCTION

Pathé and other studios produced sophisticated comedy adapted from stage plays in 1929. Reproduced from an ad in "Theatre Magazine."

In the final scene Ray Milland and Jean Arthur embrace for *Easy Living* (1937). Luis Alberni (centre) and Franklin Pangborn (right).

In *Nothing Sacred* (1937) Fredric March's clutch of the girl, Carole Lombard, causes the pair to fall in the river.

Hazel Flagg (Miss Lombard) reveals that she has been feigning a fatal illness in *Nothing Sacred*. Walter Connolly and March (standing behind her).

Publicity still (*circa* 1933) of Mae West.

Another posed shot by Miss West.

Miss West in *My Little Chickadee* (1940).

In *Twentieth Century* (1934) John Barrymore as Oscar Jaffe becomes jealous of a rival director (Charles Lane) who receives the attentions of movie queen Lilly Garland (Carole Lombard).

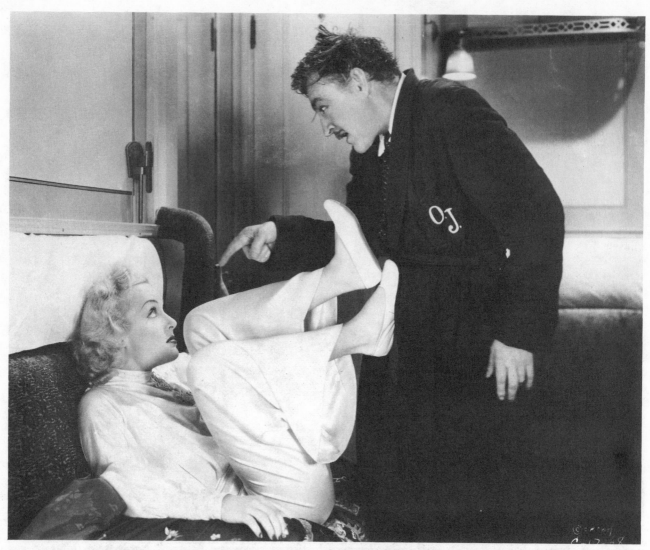

Miss Lombard and Barrymore engage in the male-female physical fight in *Twentieth Century* that was to be a common occurrence in the screwball comedy.

Eugene Pallette, Carole Lombard and Alice Brady watch Mischa Auer as Carlo executes his monkey imitation in *My Man Godfrey* (1936).

A publicity still of Carole Lombard, the most talented
actress of the sophisticated comedy.

First in a series of pictures, *The Thin Man* (1934) starred Myrna Loy and William Powell as the urbane Nora and Nick Charles.

After the Thin Man (1936) showing the principals of the series, Powell and Miss Loy, attending a wrestling match.

Roland Young as Cosmos Topper and Cary Grant as Nick Kirby in *Topper* (1937) settle down for more than one drink.

Robert Donat and Jean Park in the 1936 René Clair production, *The Ghost Goes West.*

Adapted from the stage play by Philip Barry, *Holiday* in 1938 featured Edward Everett Horton, Jean Dixon, Cary Grant, Katharine Hepburn, and Lew Ayres.

Two well-known players, Clark Gable and Constance
Bennett, appeared in sophisticated comedies like
After Office Hours (1935).

8
Folksy, Middle Class, and Sentimental

Developed by British playwrights and novelists early in the Eighteenth century, the sentimental comedy employed warmth and charm in its *persona*. Thus, humorous characters were written with many life-like facets that were lacking in most dramas of antiquity. On the other hand, this mode, which influenced the slow rise of realism in the Nineteenth century, at times undercut the main ingredients of comedy. By embracing the virtues of the common man and directing audience sympathy to portraits of the average person, the playwrights engendered a form that was light and even bland in its humour. Few laughs can be promoted from such a drama—only chuckles and smiles. Sentimental comedy can become the antithesis of the broader *genres* of farce, burlesque, and satire that poke fun at the foibles of man. Time also can be unkind to the genteel form because attitudes and values change with each age. What was funny in a past work fades as society changes. *Love Finds Andy Hardy* (1938), for example, reflected some of the attitudes toward love held by young people in their late teens during the Thirties, but it seems more suited to people in their early teens today.

Over three decades ago the genteel comedy focused on the old and young generations. More prominent in the early Thirties was the folksy comedy that dealt with the life of the middle age person. Will Rogers, Marie Dressler, and Wallace Beery were very popular during this period. Marie Dressler won an Oscar for her leading role portrayal in the sentimental comedy *Min and Bill* in 1930. Never an award winner, Will Rogers received all his adulation from a public that loved him. And he became such a money maker for Fox Film Corporation that he seemed to promote a major movement, the folksy, all-American, true-blue, light comedy.

Will Rogers had appeared in silent pictures as early as 1918 after working in vaudeville as a homespun, yet independent-souled, cowboy rope spinner who punctuated his novelty turn with wisecrack asides to the audience. Obviously, the full range of his comic abilities was not realised in the silents, and he began starring in variety shows that toured the country and played on Broadway. In 1929 Rogers returned to Hollywood and appeared in Fox's *They Had to See Paris;* he continued with the studio until his death in an airplane accident in 1935.

By 1930 this folksy comedian began to score successfully as a motion picture actor. He re-created the protagonist role of the stage comedy *Lightnin'*, a show that had brought Frank Bacon good notices on Broadway. The total film focuses on a middle-aged owner of a hotel who contemplates divorcing his wife in order to return the property—to keep it from the clutches of scoundrels. In a light way the play pokes fun at the complications of divorce and the institution of marriage. By 1933 Rogers had appeared in ten features with scripts designed to fit a character that was not far from Will's own personality—a diamond-in-the-rough, common-sense sage who loved life and most people he met. And such a man was a match for the dishonest who attempted to bilk his friends or relatives.

State Fair (1933), directed by Henry King, was one of Rogers's great hits. Adapted from a novel by Phil Strong, the film stressed the warm, rural life of the Abel Frake family. The comedian, as head of the family, played a good-natured Iowa farmer whose ambition in life was to win the blue ribbon at the fair with his best hog, Blue Boy. Light humour that would evoke chuckles developed when the human-like animal became love sick through a restricted affair with the sow in the next pen. Abel Frake also underwent many minor difficulties with his wife, son, and daughter, which promoted gentle laughter. The picture was an ode to the simple, honest, good people of our land. Although he went close to the brink of the maudlinly sentimental, director King kept a firmer hand on the material than the creators of the musical re-makes of the film by Twentieth Century-Fox in 1945 and 1962. But, most of all, these later versions did not have the strong personality of Will Rogers in the role of the father.

Following *State Fair* the next year, 1934, *David Harum* was a work that could serve as a model of the whole mode of the sentimental comedy that employs an older man or woman as a protagonist. All the characteristics of this type of film become evident when the overall plotting of the work, the dramatic *persona,* and the dialogue are examined.

With a story set in a small New England town called Homeville and a plot that revolves around events in the life of a friendly and shrewd banker named David Harum, the thematic bias for the simple world of the past becomes evident. A bachelor, David (Will Rogers), lives in the family house with his unwed, middle-aged sister, Polly. Both are devoted to each other's welfare but extend their attentions to assisting others. David becomes involved in matchmaking for young Annie (enacted by Evelyn Venable) in her attempts to catch a young man (Kent Taylor) who has come to Harum's bank to learn the trade. Therefore, the character portrayed by Rogers becomes a "Mr. Fixit," a common central character employed in the plotting of the sentimental comedy. In this film the Mr. Fixit cleverly arranges for the young couple to take a buggy ride using a horse that's a balker—a horse that eventually will stop and refuse to move. True to form, the animal refuses to budge while out in the country, and the potential lovers begin a relationship that leads to marriage. The rest of the film concerns this affair, the professional career of the young man, and a climactic race with harness horses.

David Harum is portrayed by Rogers as a personable country banker in his late fifties who is basically an honest man with a huge heart. But, in business matters David has a practical streak which reveals his shrewdness and wry humour. Engaged in a game of pool with a business man

who wonders how Harum keeps going in his little bank during a recession, David replies:

> Well, I go a long way on a man's character and I go a longer way on his collateral. And if he's got character and collateral both, I let him have about half *(he pauses, shoots a ball into the pocket)* what he asks for.

David is humble and avoids pretensions. He is asked to a formal party by a servant of a wealthy man who brings along the proper attire with the invitation. With gentle sarcasm David refuses the clothes: "Mr. Harum's compliments to General Woolsey. You tell him all I need for the dinner is an appetite. *(Adding sharply)* Got that?" With his humility, therefore, exists a crusty pride—an individualism in personal dress and manners. Individualism is more a private thing, however. In national politics he is moderately conservative. He defends the political establishment with the view that the country is "bigger than any man."

A minor fault in character, or what could more properly be called a foible, often becomes the focus of comedy in the sentimental work. David has a bit of the "dog eat dog" in his ethical system when it comes to his greatest weakness—the love of horse trading and horse racing. The best humour of the film develops when Harum deviates from the golden rule. "It's different with horse trading," drawls David, "Do to the other fellow what he'd do to you, but do it first." When his friend Annie points out that it's not Christian to get the best of a church deacon in this type of trade he observes wryly, his eyes sparkling: "When you got a balker to dispose of, you can't pick and choose. First come, first served. That's my motto."

When the practical, crusty, small town banker deals with John, the young man learning a trade, he wants to make certain the living quarters are not too comfortable. Knowing that the local hotel has poor facilities, he tests the sincerity of his apprentice by sending him there when the young man first arrives. David uses a humorous, homey analogy in describing the situation to his sister: "Well, I calculate a certain amount of fleas is good for a dog. It keeps him from worrying about being a dog."

Two sides of David Harum's personality seem in conflict, but they reveal something about our society's values in a genteel, humorous way. The banker refuses to foreclose a mortgage on a widow and gives her a Christmas present of a paid up loan. But he makes sure the good deal is not revealed because he feels it would ruin his image as a cagey, hard-headed businessman. A mild-mannered fellow who generally engages in nothing more violent than swatting a fly on his office desk, David is forced into a fist fight which he approaches with child-like glee. He comes out the winner and tells his young apprentice, "You can't expect a lot of fun like that every morning, you know." Contradictory traits of this nature not only provide comedy but illustrate the mildness of sentimental comedy. Satire, of course, hits at faults of character which often harm others, but the foibles of the sentimental figure in drama often make him more life-like and lovable. Warmth and dimension of character result—a wry, kind look at life that, at its best, has a great deal of charm.

The picture *David Harum* exhibited, in addition to its genteel humour, a broader form of entertainment that might be said to be unkind. The Negro comic, Stepin Fetchit, acts as a groom for David's horses and is traded as a "throw in" with the various dealings throughout the town. This black is a stereotype of the shiftless, slow thinking, and slow talking Negro. The humour seems more cutting now than it did at the time; such ethnic wit in the Thirties appeared in all forms of comedy. Stepin Fetchit gave the portrayal the full treatment, and his nearly unintelligible, whining complaints about some task he had to perform provided strong humour. When the character has to chase a horse, he comes back from the long hike with feet which he characterises as feeling "like they got a toothache." While he is soaking his feet, fully engrossed in his misery, his nagging wife chides him for using the hot water that she had slated for washing dishes. He points to the tub, and the dishes are revealed soaking in the same water as his feet. In a moronish, expressionless whine he observes that he is "killing two stones with one bird."

Some of the mildest humour in *David Harum* develops from the relationship of the two young lovers. No dialogue is worthy of quotation, but this type of humour evolves as we realise that the woman is more aggressive than the man in matters of love—a typical touch of so many man-woman relationships in both the sentimental and sophisticated comic films of the Thirties.

With the death of Will Rogers in 1935, one of the best comedians of the sentimental mode was lost to the age. It is hard to say how far he could have progressed with this type of drama in the films. A close examination reveals some deficiencies in his histrionic art. Will was more of a personality actor, and he generally used what he had rather than adapt to the part. His Oklahoma accent worked fairly well in *State Fair* but seemed inaccurate for the Yankee character in *David Harum*. The same could be said of the 1931 *A Connecticut Yankee*. Nevertheless, the charm of his personality made up for defects of this type. He presented a part of the American character that was rich in human values.

Marie Dressler and Wallace Beery also portrayed some aspects of our national culture. Two works, *Min and Bill* (1930) and *Tugboat Annie* (1933), starred this excellent pair in some of the best acted roles of the period. Viewed today, these films are a reminder of the wealth of solid, skilled character actors like Miss Dressler and Beery who starred in movies four decades ago.

There is an earthiness in the two old seaside characters, Min and Bill, that makes the movie one of the most interesting examples of the sentimental mode. Lovable, lower-class characters, they reflect a human directness toward the problems of life that would not exist in the middle-class comedy of the late Thirties. Marie Dressler and Wallace Berry portray these roles of two crude people with many faults but honest hearts.

As in many sentimental comedies, *Min and Bill* incorporates serious story material and is designed for chuckles rather than laughs. Min acts as a mother for a young girl she has raised from infancy. She protects her and tries to send her to a "finishing" school by digging into her life savings. When the true mother of the girl, a prostitute, threatens to reveal the truth of the girl's origin in order to gain money, Min is forced into a fight and kills the prostitute. Thus Min faces jail to preserve the happiness of the girl.

While the basic plot of *Min and Bill* is not comic, there is an overall treatment of character and many situations that becomes humorous. There is an elaborate comic fight between Min and Bill, for example, that contrasts sharply with similar physical fights by lovers in the screwball or madcap comedies. Alcoholic Bill has been caught by Min in an affair with another woman. A war horse of a woman, she beats him up. Although this amiable old soak could best her in a fight, he has a code of honour toward women that restricts him. He refuses to lift a hand as she throws anything she can lift at him and beats him with her fists. When Bill hides from her blows in a closet, Min smashes the door down with a fire axe. Min's *coup de grâce* is achieved with a huge water pitcher. When he revives from the blow, a reconciliation of the couple puts the finishing touches to this comic scene. By contrast the sophisticated comedy depicted a comic physical fight with an equal exchange of punches; usually the fight between male and female ended in a draw.

In 1933 *Tugboat Annie* became a replay of the same type of old codgers with Miss Dressler and Berry playing opposite each other once more. As in *Min and Bill* they are characters with barnacles on the outside and sweet chocolate on the inside. In *Tugboat Annie* the role enacted by Miss Dressler is depicted as more aggressive because the dipsomania of her husband, Terry, causes her more difficulty than in the former film. Annie becomes the captain who does her best under trying circumstances with her unreliable husband who works under her command. In one delightful scene she tries to solve a social situation at a formal reception by snatching glasses of punch from her husband. Naturally, she drinks more than her husband and joins him in his state of inebriation. But, as in *Min and Bill*, a good portion of the plot is serious and sentimental.

Another, less significant type of sentimental comedy developed when Hollywood drew up popular radio favourites to act in films. Kate Smith, noted for her singing and chatty manner as a radio star, appeared in *Hello, Everybody!* in 1933. It was the industry's attempt to transfer the magnetic personality of the aural medium to the visual medium. But Kate was better heard than seen. The material they designed for her did not help. Hollywood devised sentimental comedy plot material for her. As *Time* magazine put it, she spent much of her time on the farm "crooning to horses and pigs." When not engaging in this strange world of the variety and musical show, she became a Miss Fixit and crusaded for farmers by raising money to win a court battle by her bucolic friends against a power company that attempted to build a dam that would eliminate many acres of rich farm land. Kate gets the money by singing professionally. Only one of many radio personalities who appeared in films during the Thirties, Miss Smith's charm was vocal. She was an awkward actress and only succeeded as a dealer in sentimental songs. Even Fibber McGee and Molly, who were adept in half-hour, sentimental comedy dramas on radio, could not succeed with the visual medium.

A very important influence on the increasing

number of folksy and genteel comedies in the late Thirties came about when public pressure created a strong code of ethics for all the producers in Hollywood during 1934. There were strong seeds of sentimentalism in so many pictures at the time. But censorship cut the effectiveness of sharp comedy of licence—comedy used by such personalities as Mae West. With an elimination or watering down of sexual repartee, the producers over-reacted and moved to the creation of "wholesome" family entertainment. This attitude developed in Hollywood's embrace of the classics, adaptations from literature (usually the novel) which were approved reading in secondary schools throughout the country. At the time this meant novels from the Nineteenth century or Shakespeare. Dickens was a favourite and was sometimes effectively rendered by good adaptations and strong acting. *David Copperfield* (1935), for example, was this type of movie. Such stars as Roland Young, W. C. Fields, Lionel Barrymore, and Edna Mae Oliver provided the necessary support for the somewhat saccharin leads to make the picture a worthy, entertaining effort. The comic elements of the movie are true to the mode of Charles Dickens's sentimentalism.

Even the movie adaptation of Shakespeare's *A Midsummer Night's Dream* displayed some of the good features of the Elisabethan comedy. However, the production, under the supervision of the famed German stage director, Max Reinhardt, and movie director, William Dieterle, became a milk-toast version of a classic. Romantic leads Dick Powell and Olivia de Havilland seemed to have a struggle even with this simplified version of Shakespeare. Mickey Rooney, at the age of fifteen but looking more like a nine-year-old, was an impish Puck, but the poetry of the role was mangled by this young actor who more properly seemed to be suited to *Our Gang* comedies at this stage of his development. Warner Brothers also used a battery of comedians to portray the village players: Hugh Herbert, Frank McHugh, Arthur Treacher, and Joe E. Brown. James Cagney, strangely miscast, played the role of the amateur thespian, Bottom. The production was an interesting experiment and probably helped to abate the growing pressure to censor the industry. It probably convinced some moralist that Hollywood was at last providing "proper" fare for its audiences.

Two earlier films that helped to set the tone of the genteel movement on a serious and comic level were released late in 1933 when the clamour for reform in the cinema was reaching a peak.

Little Women, adapted from the novel by Louisa May Alcott, provided the necessary heart throbs for those who liked sentimental drama of a serious nature. Paramount opened its campaign to appease middle-class morality and culture with a screen version of *Alice in Wonderland.* As in many of these experiments to support and stimulate the patronage of the moral uplifters, the studio unleashed an all star cast for the enterprise. Some important comedians of the period had very short bits: Leon Errol appeared as Uncle Gilbert; Ned Sparks as Caterpillar; Sterling Holloway as Frog-Footman; Alison Skipworth as Duchess; Jack Oakie as Tweedledum, and W. C. Fields as Humpty Dumpty. The more prominent parts of Queen of Hearts, Mad Hatter, and White Knight were enacted by May Robson, Edward Everett Horton, and Gary Cooper. All actors were loaded down in elaborate costumes, well caked with make-up, or decked with elaborate masks. The name of the game became "Guess who is playing whom or what." This may account for some of the problem in the work as it is viewed through today's perspective. By voice identification, for instance, one can recognise the familiar clipped accent and voice patterns of Cary Grant encased in a shell as he attempts to render the lines of Mock Turtle. All of this adds up to a painfully laboured venture. Director Norman Z. McLeod couldn't achieve the free-flowing, wry mood necessary to make this comedy a worthy production.

Comedy classics like *Alice in Wonderland* reflected the beginnings of a strong move to the sentimental film drama. Works of this type had some virtues but too often seemed to compromise with the taste of the time—to reduce a literary classic to a level that would appeal to the child. In fact, if there is any doubt that such an appeal was being made, we need only look at the growing tide of movies with moppet heroines produced at that time.

The darling of the sentimental comedy of the period was Shirley Temple. She was in feature films by the time she was four years old and attracted wide attention in Educational Pictures' *Baby Burlesks* and *Frolics of Youth* series, two-reelers with stories centred on the special talents and exploits of children. Even after considerable success in features such as *Little Miss Marker* and *Bright Eyes* in 1934, she appeared in two-reelers for Educational.

While many two-reel comedies of the period concentrated on broad farce, Shirley Temple's *Pardon My Pups* employed light, humorous plot lines involving a family situation. A little girl, Mary Lou, picks up a stray dog and tries to give him a bath. A sentimental conflict develops when her father decides he will not have a mongrel because he wants a pure bred hunting dog for his own. To save the dog from being "put to sleep" Shirley hides it in a shack and steals food from her mother's kitchen. A fantastic clinching gag develops when Mary Lou feeds her pet spaghetti, and the animal accidentally starts chewing the strands of a sweater in its basket, thinking it is the same thing as the food. The dog gives birth to pups attired in tiny little sweaters. In a climactic fight with a smart alec boy Mary Lou helps her brother win by sticking a fork in the rear of the boy villain. But slapstick and violence seldom intruded to spice the genteel comedy. Shirley Temple usually enacted the role of a sweet little girl who seldom hated anyone. Rising to stardom as the cute kid, Shirley had an international fan club that boasted about four million members.

Nine of Miss Temple's features were released in 1934, a fact that indicates the grinding pace of some studio productions in the Thirties. *Little Miss Marker* was a sentimental story of Damon Runyon origin. In the work Shirley is raised by a bookie named Sorrowful Jones (Adolphe Menjou). The comedy evolves by placing the little girl in the tough, fast-paced world of horse racing and gambling. Sentiment is created when she is thrown by a horse and has to undergo surgery. *Bright Eyes,* released late in 1934, introduces a playmate for Shirley. The playmate is enacted by Jane Withers, a child actress who would soon become a star in her own pictures. In *Bright Eyes* Shirley brings tears to the audience when she learns of her mother's death, and she serves as a Miss Fixit by arranging a reconciliation between an aviator and his girl. As in most of her pictures, she also has opportunities to sing several songs.

When she found a dance partner with the charm and skills of Bill Robinson in the 1935 productions *The Little Colonel* and *The Littlest Rebel,* she displayed increasing talent for song and dance routines. This appealed to a public that didn't mind the vaudeville turn which had little to do with the plot. Of course, the story lines of these films were filled with the *clichés* of the Civil war sentimental drama, and the humour was very, very light. It also didn't seem to bother the public who liked such fluff that laughter and tears seldom mix very well.

Because the system moulded her as a child-star, it took great pains to tailor her films to her talents. In all three of her 1938 creations, Shirley plays a little girl who engages in show business in the climactic part of the movie. With each film a standard pattern emerges—in the case of these pictures the link with the musical comedy becomes more evident. Sentiment reigns. In each film the little girl is deprived of a mother, and emotional response from the audience is assured. Sentiment and light humour develop from her attitudes toward farm life in *Rebecca of Sunnybrook Farm*, a band of out-of-work actors in *Little Miss Broadway*, and various characters in a big city apartment in *Just Around the Corner*. Each plot features Shirley as the protagonist who "wins the day" with a plan or subterfuge directed against those stuffy, conservative people who make life difficult for a little girl. Films of this nature exist in the mythical or daydream world of Nancy Drew and Tom Swift. Shirley, like the superteenagers of these popular adventure stories, is a clever girl who can take action and solve her problems and the problems of adults in a world controlled by people four to seven times her age.

Another Miss Fixit moppet appeared in a feature film *Handle with Care* in 1932 when she was six years old. Jane Withers was an important child star by the time she appeared in her tenth film, *Pepper* (1936), with comedians Irvin S. Cobb and Slim Summerville. But Jane never reached Shirley Temple's popularity. Working for the same studio, Fox, she seemed to be assigned to lower budget pictures than Shirley. She also played a different character; Jane was more of the rascal— the little girl who would take delight in a practical joke. The titles of some of her works, *The Holy Terror* (1937), *Rascals* (1938), and *Always in Trouble* (1938) indicate the type of comic character she portrayed. In *Rascals,* for example, Jane plays a girl who obtains money for an operation to restore the romantic lead's (Rochelle Hudson) memory after an automobile accident. To obtain the funds, she and her teenage friends put pepper in the horns of the regular band and take over a concert-dance with their own harmonica band.

Jane Withers's movies, like Shirley Temple's, have not worn well with time. They offer only unique child actresses with interesting personalities; the acting and the plotting of such vehicles are slight—the comedy of even the best scenes has faded. The comic stories created for both these girls are not much better than situation comedies written for a TV series in the Fifties and Sixties.

By 1938 the moppet and teenage stars were firmly established; older comedians like Bob Burns in *The Arkansas Traveler* were poor substitutes for the magnetism of Will Rogers. An invasion of family comedy was clearly a trend of the times. In 1939 Frank Vreeland claimed that the madcap comedies had run their cycle and that the public wanted "unaffected naturalism." In a book sympathetic to this trend, *Foremost Films of 1938,* he applauded it as a basically honest movement:

> That simplicity and spontaneity led to the rise of the family picture, dealing with everyday folks who had familiar troubles. Thus 1938 will pass into screen history as the period when photoplays featuring ma, pa and the children became the vogue. They shot to top rank at the box office. This unpretentious type was inaugurated by "The Jones Family" . . .

Vreeland evidently refers to the 1937 Twentieth Century-Fox productions, *The Jones Family in Big Business* and *The Jones Family in Hot Water,* cinematic renderings of characters from the popular fiction creations of Katharine Kavanaugh. While critic Vreeland avoids the snobbery often employed by evaluators of the film who berate anything that has popular appeal, his views seem too general and too patronising of the age. He overrates *Love Finds Andy Hardy,* a work that has many of the ingredients of the genre. He finds "realistic" and even "naturalistic" touches in this work although we now can see the writing, directing and acting as thin and artificial. He sees the picture as a valid reflection of the time:

> The story touches off to the right degree the enormous importance which adolescence gives to attending a country club dance, and the appalling loss of caste from going stag. It highlights the latest fads of youth that denote this age—the craving of boys to own cars of their own, even cheap jalopies, and their desire to be seen only with girls who are "sensational."

Vreeland found this comedy charming and heartwarming. But attitudes change, and the film's views of adolescence now seem thin and even a bit foolish. Typical of this genteel humour was a low keyed discussion between Andy Hardy (Mickey Rooney) and his father (Lewis Stone):

ANDY: Dad, can I talk to you man to man?
JUDGE: That's the way I always want it to be.
ANDY: Man to man, can a guy be in love with two girls at once?
JUDGE: Both estimable young ladies?

ANDY: Aw, we do a little kissing and hugging. But it's all good clean fun—you know—like me and Polly.
JUDGE: Object matrimony?
ANDY: Matrimony! Oh, Dad, you don't have to worry. I'm never going to get married—ever.
JUDGE: That's a momentous decision.
ANDY: Not until I'm middle-aged—twenty-five or twenty-six.
JUDGE: Sound idea.

Attempts by the adolescent Polly (Ann Rutherford) to be sophisticated and adult are gently spoofed by the screenwright. However, Andy gets pleasure from physical contact even though it is obviously very limited. The following exchange illustrates the mild amusement which results from the two contrasting attitudes:

POLLY: Really, I think we're getting much too old for that sort of thing—hugging and kissing.
ANDY: I ain't ever going' to get too old for huggin' and kissin'.

Humour through the plot line is revealed in *Love Finds Andy Hardy* when Andy becomes entangled with three girls. Judy Garland (at this time a very young looking sixteen-year-old) plays the twelve-year-old Betsy who pines for older teenage boys. Her yearnings provide some of the best light humour. Andy treats Betsy as a younger sister even in the face of many manipulations she attempts in order to gain his affection. One of the three songs incorporated in the picture describes Betsy's plight when she sings "In Between"—meaning that she is too old to be a child and too young to be an object of love. Like the moppets in the many movies of Shirley Temple and Jane Withers, Betsy becomes the Miss Fixit who solves other people's problems. Betsy manoeuvres cleverly and gets Andy into the arms of the proper girl.

Most family comedies exhibited patterns similar to those found in the Andy Hardy films. Even in the Sixties the popular, sentimental *Father Knows Best* series on television indicated that the *genre* was still accepted by the public. The parents in this type of work are usually exemplary figures. Judge Hardy and his wife provide only a few gentle, more embracing than provoking remarks when they observe the minor pitfalls of their offspring as the youngsters struggle with problems of popularity and love. The parents are sweet, lovable, and completely faultless.

There were exceptions to this pattern of middle-class, sentimental comedy. Deanna Durbin's *That Certain Age* (1938) dealt with the country club set. Miss Durbin's Alice Fuller in the film provided a humorous look at a teenager falling in love with an older man, Vincent Bullit, played by Melvyn Douglas. The film has a plot that ranges between the sophisticated and sentimental comedy. The worried father tries to blacken the heroic image Alice has of Vincent by indicating that he drinks too much and lives too fast a life. The daughter counters the father's attempt by declaring she will help Vincent conquer his vices. In comic frustration the father points out the difference in age between them: "Stop worrying about that stiff—I've known him all my life." Undaunted, Alice exclaims, "Gee, Daddy, have you? You're lucky!"

But the scenes with another teenager (Jackie Cooper) and Alice are genteel and sentimental. As in so many films of the period, musical elements are incorporated. Miss Durbin was noted more for her light opera singing voice than for her acting. In *That Certain Age* she sings songs for guests in her family's mansion—usually at the request of the father who is proud of his daughter's talent.

Another work, *The Young in Heart* (1938), also reflected this unusual combination of sophisticated wit and sentimental humour. The film features a family of bilkers who make a living by robbing the rich after obtaining a foothold in a wealthy household. The offspring, a young man and girl, become disgusted with their parents when they gain the confidence of a rich woman whom they like. The parents, played by Roland Young and Billie Burke, also develop a soft spot for the woman they intended to cheat. This switch of heart throws the last part of the work into a genteel vein, producing something like the rake reformed, a type of comedy that evolved in the early part of Eighteenth century English theatre when sentimentalism began its undermining of the more risible Restoration comedy.

In February of 1938 RKO Radio Pictures released one of the most unusual variations on the comedies of the period. *Snow White and the Seven Dwarfs* was Walt Disney's first feature length cartoon film. A product of many talents, artists, sequence directors, supervising animators, story adaptors, music and sound effects people, this movie was an immediate success. Its run at the Radio City Music Hall grossed nearly half a million dollars, and the dialogue was translated into eleven languages, making it an international success. While the work contains many slapstick elements in sequences with the animals and with the dwarfs, the overall tone is sentimental. The basic plot of a Cinderella story holds the total work together, and the love songs, "Some Day My Prince Will Come," "I'm Wishing," and "One Song," reinforce the sentimental nature of the work. The relation of the dwarfs to Snow White also provides lighter comedy. The stereotype traits of each dwarf often provide the broader, more laughable comedy of the picture. The names Dopey, Bashful, Grumpy, Happy, Sneezey, and Sleepy indicate the traits being used to gain laughs. Doc, the leader of the group, transposes sounds and gets very confused as he urges his band to investigate their own house for an intruder. He says "Careful men, search every cook 'n nanny . . . uh . . . hook 'n granny . . . crooked fan . . . search everywhere."

Walt Disney Enterprises has re-released *Snow White and the Seven Dwarfs* many times since 1938. Adults who saw the work as children now can take their own daughters or sons (or even grandchildren) to see the work. Adults, you may be sure, also enjoy the work. The animation and the abstraction of fantasy itself prevent the work from aging too much even though the sentiment of Disney's works may eventually work its toll.

Released late in 1938, *You Can't Take It with You* is a family comedy that ranks among the best of the genteel films of the age. From the pens of George S. Kaufman and Moss Hart, this Pulitzer Prize-winning play enjoyed a two-year Broadway run. Columbia Pictures paid $200,000 for screen rights and contracted Frank Capra as director and Robert Riskin as screenwright for the work. The director and adaptor skilfully handled the material, but created a sentimentalisation of the stage version of the play. Nevertheless, the wacky family, the Sycamores, plus their friends, are still amusing characters. The alteration of the original script was not enough to reduce the whole situation to the saccharin world of Judge Hardy, Andy, and the synthetic, Hollywood small town of family comedies.

The eccentric nature of the Sycamore family in *You Can't Take It with You* shows some borrowing from the sophisticated comedy of characters who want to "do their own thing." Frank Vreeland (in *Foremost Films of 1938*, p. 135) quotes from the screenplay as the young lovers, Alice Sycamore (Jean Arthur), and Tony Kirby (James Stewart) express their views on the family and friends:

TONY: Living with them must be like living in a world that Walt Disney might have thought of.
ALICE: We haven't Donald Duck, or Mickey Mouse, or Snow White. Do you like them, Tony?
TONY: I'm mad about them. Everyone does just what he wants to do.
ALICE: Grandpa started it thirty-five years ago. He suddenly quit business one day. Started up in the elevator—came right down again—and never went back. He could have been a rich man. But he said he wasn't having any fun. He began collecting stamps because that's what he likes best. Now he's an expert and gets paid just to appraise collections. Dad makes fireworks because there's a sense of excitement about it. And Mother—know why Mother writes plays? (*Alice smiles*) Because eight years ago a typewriter was delivered to the house by mistake.

Vreeland's quote from the scenario reveals some updating of the script by its reference to Walt Disney and the cartoon feature *Snow White and the Seven Dwarfs*. Grandpa is less eccentric than he was portrayed on the stage. The original script described him as collecting snakes and going to graduation ceremonies. There is a retention of some of the invective humour that existed in the original work when the morose Russian ballet teacher (played by Mischa Auer) discusses some of the symptoms of the rich druge, Mr. Kirby (Edward Arnold), who suffers the stresses of his all business and no play life:

KOLENKHOV: Perhaps it's not indigestion at all, Mr. Kirby. Perhaps it is stomach ulcers.
GRANDPA: You mustn't mind Mr. Kolenkhov. He's Russian—and Russians are inclined to look on the dark side.
KOLENKHOV: All right, I'm a Russian. But a friend of mine, a Russian, died from stomach ulcers.
PENNY: Please, Mr. Kirby has indigestion and that's all!
KOLENKHOV: (*Shrugging ominously*) All right, let him wait!

The total work expresses a desire for freedom, a similar theme of madcap comedy, but does not go as far with comic licence as the sophisticated mode does. Jokes at the expense of others were seldom used in the Capra-Riskin version of the play. In fact, in the fashion of folksy comedy it embraces nearly everyone. A spirit of comradeship is kindled between rich and poor when the wealthy Kirby learns the simple values of enjoying life. In the end he abandons his stuffy attitudes and joins the Sycamores and their friends. At the fade-out he engages in a harmonica duet with Grandpa (Lionel Barrymore).

The concept of a reformation or a change in values was common in the sentimental comedy. It was generally an embrace of *status quo* or a move to somewhat moderate middle-class morals and values. The freedom that the Sycamores practice was a virtue in the depression years—almost a rationalisation for being out of work or not working was devised by the controlling comic idea. A change in status and values was best expressed by the most admirable film in this style, *Ruggles of Red Gap*.

In the "Literary Digest" of March 23, 1935 *Ruggles of Red Gap* was given a rave review. British actor Charles Laughton had scored a success in comedy after he had gained popular and critical success in serious roles in the films *The Private Life of Henry VIII* and *The Barretts of Wimpole Street*. "Argus," the reviewer for the "Literary Digest," described Laughton's portrait of Ruggles as "mellow, straightforward, and, when humour is required, hilarious. It probably is the best characterisation he yet has brought to the screen."

This film is also memorable for the excellent handling of a contrast between two ways of life— the formal existence of a British butler and the rugged, personal life of a United States cattleman. The services of Ruggles, the butler, are acquired by the American (played by actor Charles Ruggles) who wins the domestic from Lord George Van Bassingwell (Roland Young) in a poker game. Egbert Froud, the cattle baron, changes Ruggles's total way of living. Egbert treats him as an equal, much to the butler's disgust, and forces Ruggles to drink with him. Both master and servant end up drunk. Stiff and silly when inebriated, Charles Laughton deftly plays a highly comic scene as he depicts the butler still trying to maintain his role but periodically breaking forth with a "Whoopee!" A man more cultivated than most of his masters in all the arts of a sophisticated life, Ruggles believes in keeping his place. Some of the reversal of roles comedy achieved by James Barrie in his 1902 stage play, *The Admirable Crichton*, seems to be operating in this film. Ruggles, like the butler Crichton, is a superior being who, in certain circumstances, takes charge. Ruggles tries not to display his distaste for some of the ignorance and the crudities of his new master and mistress. The wife, Effie Froud (Mary Boland), for example, hears Ruggles use the word "indubitably" and gushes, "What beautiful French you speak, Ruggles!"

Early in the film, the cattle baron puts the seed of the butler's conversion in Ruggles's mind. When Egbert has to force his newly acquired "gentleman's man" to sit with him and have a drink in a Parisian café, the cattleman points out, "You're as good as I am and I as good as you are, ain't I?" The butler agrees but remains in his detached role as long as he remains sober. A good part of the comedy develops because Ruggles becomes frustrated when he cannot function in his accustomed way. Equality, before his big change, is a distasteful way of life.

A case of mistaken identity, ironically, leads to Ruggles's transformation. The Red Gap newspaper erroneously reports him to be a British Colonel. The Frouds must go along with the mistake or be shunned by this rugged, pioneer town that is looking for any respectable or famous person to give prestige to the local community.

Sentiment develops when Ruggles leaves the employment of the Frouds. In a saloon he is the only one in the establishment who can give the message delivered by Lincoln at Gettysburg. He recites the speech perfectly because he has committed it to memory, believing it to be very important in a "land of opportunity." In the hands of a less accomplished actor this scene would be mawkish, but Laughton underplays beautifully, and director Leo McCarey assists him by keeping the other actors' reactions on a simple level with a warm touch.

Throughout the drama Egbert has begrudgingly allowed himself to be pushed into high society. To his wife he asserts his independence in a way that emphasises the overall comic theme. Noting that Ruggles has taught him that all men are created equal, he declares that he doesn't want to live a fancy, artificial life—that he must be himself. "Men are created equal to women," Egbert observes. "That's why you have no right to order me around." In the sophisticated comedy, there was seldom a return to this position. The wacky battle of the sexes seemed to continue even during the resolution, with the *status quo* never being achieved. But in *Ruggles of Red Gap* the man who has been made ridiculous by going along with his wife's desires re-establishes his dominant role. In this situation we can observe another trait of the sentimental form.

On the other hand, *Ruggles of Red Gap* has a few touches that would make suitable scenes in the sophisticated comedy. When his former British master comes to visit Ruggles to "buy him back," the reformed butler, who now owns a restaurant, expresses his newly developed state of independence:

RUGGLES: Am I someone or am I not?
BASSINGWELL: Well, I only just got here so I wouldn't know.
RUGGLES: Oh, I am someone, my lord.
BASSINGWELL: Let me be the first one to congratulate you. How did you ever find it out?

This exchange is delivered with excellent British understatement by Laughton and Roland Young and provides some of the spice, the contrast and gamut of comedy that elevates this film to a high level.

Two of the worthiest works of this group, *Ruggles of Red Gap* and *You Can't Take It with You,* display a creative blending of various comedy styles—mainly the sentimental and the sophisticated. Such a fusion was not forced and illustrates how superior directing and acting could accomplish this blend. If other basically sentimental works had employed this method, the whole genteel style might have had more works to recommend it and many films of the Thirties might have been saved from aging. The comic theme and characterisation of both these works lean more to the sentimental, but the serious or even maudlin, emotional elements never intrude to spoil the comedy. Most of the time we can laugh with the characters and, occasionally, at them. Such control of the comedy and such a combination was rare, but it produced the most laughable dramas of the species.

The sentimental comedy at its best was not easily achieved. Maybe it seemed to be a mode that could be ground out by anyone—a deceptively commercial product to fit the tastes of the time. But in order to endure, this kind of comedy needs a solid script, clever direction, and excellent acting. Much credit can be given to directors Frank Capra and Leo McCarey; they obviously had a feel for their material, and by their creative efforts they gave the form a higher rank in the gamut of comedy.

Wallace Beery and Marie Dressler were teamed in roles that were similar in both *Min and Bill* (1930) and *Tugboat Annie* (1933).

Will Rogers, Lew Ayres, and Janet Gaynor in posed still for *State Fair* (1933).

In *State Fair* the roles of Melissa and Abel Frake were enacted by Louise Dresser and Rogers.

Banker Will Rogers and his apprentice, Kent Taylor, in *David Harum* (1934).

Rogers engages in "horse talk" with Noah Beery in
David Harum.

In *Curly Top* (1935) Shirley Temple with Jane Darwell
(centre), Etienne Girardot, and John Boles.

In the 1935 production *The Littlest Rebel* Miss Temple sang and danced with Bill Robinson.

Miss Temple talking with Lionel Barrymore in *The Little Colonel* (1935).

Another moppet, Jane Withers, captivated audiences in *Pepper* (1936) with Slim Summerville and Irvin S. Cobb.

In 1940 the "Andy Hardy" series continued with *Andy Hardy Meets Debutante* starring Judy Garland and Mickey Rooney.

Walt Disney's first feature length cartoon, *Snow White and the Seven Dwarfs* (1938), became the big hit of the year.

One of the best genteel comedies of the Thirties, *Ruggles of Red Gap* (1935), employed Mary Boland (left) and Charles Ruggles (right) in the roles of Effie and Egbert Froud.

9

The Latter-Day Falstaff

As if he were a gift from some ancient muse, a successful vaudeville juggler underwent a slow but sure metamorphosis to become the outstanding comedian of the sound age. W. C. Fields, like some reincarnation from the past, reminds us of a comic type who has weathered the test of the ages. There is something of the braggart soldier from Roman comedy, a strutting Capitino from the *commedia dell' arte* or Falstaff from Shakespeare's plays. But he has more than these facets. He becomes a bungling husband, harassed by his wife—a comic type that ranges from the classical Greek stage through the medieval tale, the restoration and Eighteenth century comedy, down to modern times. In short, Fields ran the gamut of humour with a multi-faceted character of his own creation—with, of course, some help from his directors. Next to him all other comics of the sound age remain two-dimensional. Appreciated in his day, he now receives praise close to adoration. While this acclaim may seem only a "camp" trend—a temporary fad of those who have recently rediscovered the artistry of this unique comedian —there is enough sober evaluation to establish his status as the comedy king of the Thirties.

Fields's introduction to the sound film proved to be a humble beginning. He had prominent roles in eleven mediocre silent screen comedies. A twenty-minute two-reeler made in 1930, *The Golf Specialist*, merely indicated that he was lifting material from one of his vaudeville routines, a sketch centered on giving golf lessons to a beautiful girl. The full potentiality of Fields's talent did not appear until he made four shorts for Mack Sennett in 1932 and 1933. He scripted the works himself and at least one film, *The Barber Shop*, can be said to contain many of the aspects of the actor's wit. A feature, *Her Majesty Love* (1931),

was not a distinguished piece, but it had the virtue of combining the talents of Leon Errol with those of Fields—an interesting combination that was not fully exploited. Obviously, he would not reach the peak of his powers until he was allowed to control the content of his own pictures. Also, he needed experience in a few features before his dramatic talents could be clearly transferred from his vaudeville heritage to the screen.

A much livelier feature than *Her Majesty Love, Million Dollar Legs* (1932) had the advantage of imitating the silent screen tradition. But a copy grafted with voiced gags could not be the real thing, and it now remains a curious bit of nostalgia, almost an ode to the dead art that seemed to be kept alive in its true form by the daring Chaplin who refused to switch to sound until 1940. Unfortunately, *Million Dollar Legs* was not a vehicle for Fields. Had it been so, the work might have been an outstanding comedy. It was more of a "Grand Hotel" of comics, old and new. The new breed, Jack Oakie, Hugh Herbert, and Billy Gilbert had prominent roles. Hank Mann, Ben Turpin, and Andy Clyde played minor parts —almost symbolically indicating the future of the silent screen comedian.

As if to show its loyalty to vintage humour, *Million Dollar Legs* opens with a corny title gag superimposed (with each line appearing one after another) over a view of a mid European town:

Klopstokia . . . a far away country
Chief Export . . . Goats and Nuts
Chief Imports . . . Goats and Nuts
Chief Inhabitants . . . Goats and Nuts

And this title almost sums up the wacky character of the whole picture.

In the opening scene George Barbier, playing

the role of a brash manufacturer declares: "I want to get out of this country. I have a feeling I'm being spied on." Told not to worry because spying could not be possible in Klopstokia, the magnate doesn't see, pressing close behind him, the cross-eyed Ben Turpin with obvious cloak and dagger garb—a large brimmed, black hat and a long cape. In such dress he appears periodically throughout the picture, taking notes on the proceedings—a mute spectre of the silent screen comedy.

Appearing in a carriage, Fields strikes quite a figure as a dictator, even though he is called President. He growls into a dictaphone:

"My Dear General . . ." No, that's too friendly. "Dear General . . ." Still too friendly. "General Wagonhauls . . ." "Dear Son . . ." Now, why should I be so respectful? I'll demote the pup. "Corporal Wagonhauls . . ." (He laughs gleefully) He'll resent that. He'll resent anything I call him. The crud!

The tyrant finally gets so annoyed that he orders the object of his mushrooming wrath completely stripped of rank and placed under arrest. In one, brief monologue Fields establishes the comic potential of his character—an impossible authoritarian who obviously gets his "kicks" by pushing people around. Later we learn that he holds his position because he can best every member of his cabinet in the Indian wrestle. A running gag develops with Hugh Herbert, who plays the role of Secretary of the Treasury. Time after time Herbert is beaten in the contest, and he soothes his injured hand by rubbing it, pulls himself together, and mutters intensely under his breath: "Someday."

As richly as some scenes display Fieldsian humour, the picture doesn't focus enough on the comedian's antics. Jack Oakie, as the comical romantic interest, shares and often dominates a great deal of the footage of the film. In the role of a slick, not very bright, fast-talking salesman, Oakie exhibits a thin, tiny bag of comic tricks. Nevertheless, even with this limited acting vocabulary, his breezy young man has a lot of dash that gives the movie vitality.

Besides the characteristics of a film that seems to be an ode to Mack Sennett, Million Dollar Legs retains a hint of the musical comedy influence which develops with the burlesque of the femme fatale in the role of Mata Machree. Actress Lyda Roberti dances and sings of her own charms, warning all men who approach her that something drastic will happen to them, as she repeats over

and over, ". . . when I get hot." Soon after this, Oakie sings a brief Klopstokian love song which obviously is a type of double-talk. But such musical diversions are confined to these scenes.

Fields's comic tyrant has less influence on the plot as the film progresses. Oakie's character proves to be the plot mover by getting the athletic Klopstokians to enter the international Olympic games. Early in the picture we see Fields juggling medicine clubs, people, and words. But his presence and influence fade half way through the picture.

In his brief stay with Mack Sennett, producing two-reelers, Fields had nearly full control of his material. From 1932 to 1934, he appeared in many pictures—probably too many, for most of his efforts were unrewarding. But all this provided a training ground for the development of some of his best works.

In 1932 If I Had a Million was a multi-drama of short tales, with sequences for such personalities as Gary Cooper, George Raft, Charles Laughton, and Wynne Gibson. One of the sequences from the film featured Fields and Alison Skipworth as husband and wife who have their new car demolished by a careless driver. Inheriting a million dollars, they buy a fleet of automobiles and proceed to track down "road hogs" and wreck them with their many vehicles. One by one the cars come in for replacement so that they can run into what they consider to be an offending driver. Actually, this kind of material is more suited to the talents of Harold Lloyd or Buster Keaton. They often handled similar types of situations by developing several comic variations and nuances. Fields seems to lack innovation in this work, and many developments of this situation are repetitious and mechanical.

In 1933 he appeared in three features, International House, Tillie and Gus, and Alice in Wonderland. The third work, showing Hollywood's emerging, not too successful, bout with the classics, hides W. C.'s face in an egg shell as Humpty Dumpty. In this brief appearance on the screen there is nothing distinctive about his performance. International House, in the same manner of the later Big Broadcast of 1938, has its roots in stage vaudeville and the radio variety programme of the period. A Chinese inventor, Doctor Wong, uses a "radioscope," an all-seeing but erratic form of television, to bring in various comedy skits and musical shows. Wong's addition of video to audio doesn't fare well with such radio personalities of the time as Rudy Vallee and Colonel

Stoopnagle. Fields functions as a character with only part of the plot devoted to him, and the picture seems to have been shot with many of the leading actors seldom meeting each other. Only occasionally does Fields have a chance to lash verbally the scatter-brained Gracie Allen who often engages in weak vaudeville patter with George Burns. One memorable moment develops when the comedian strolls down the hotel hallway and stops to look into a keyhole. He beautifully tosses off the line, "What will they think of next?" in a way that distinguishes his verbal humour from that of Groucho Marx. Similar "off-colour" material was used by Groucho, to be sure, but the execution would be much different in Marx's hand. He would have rolled his eyes and smirked directly at the camera.

Tillie and Gus was the first feature to focus on Fields as the leading character. It was obviously made to exploit the talents of a comedian who had gained fame—both popular and critical acclaim. But the work was not fully in the hands of Bill Fields. Director Francis Martin seemed to favour genteel comedy and didn't let the comedian unleash the complete force of his brand of invective. What might have become one of his masterpieces comes off as second rate. Nevertheless, some of the character facets that he later developed more effectively began to emerge.

Con-man qualities of Fields's screen portrayals were embryonic in this film and would be more fully exploited in *The Old Fashioned Way* (1934), *Poppy* (1936), *You Can't Cheat an Honest Man* (1939), and *My Little Chickadee* (1940). When he is forced to leave an Alaskan town for crooked gambling in *Tillie and Gus*, as Augustus Winterbottom he utters one of his pretentious, garbled statements that would soon grace many of his films: "There comes a tide in the affairs of men, my dear Blubber, when we must take the bull by the tail and face the situation." He meets an ex-wife (played by Alison Skipworth—a cooler version of the Marie Dressler type), calling her "My Little Chickadee" and "My Dove"—labels that he often employed to sweet-talk women, particularly when he had been accused by them of some misdeed. We also see him in the often repeated card game scene. Pretending to be an innocent, he declares he's drawn an ace for a dealer position without showing it to the other players. With mock surprise he discovers he's won the first hand with four aces.

Another facet of his character is less well de-

veloped. Fields's dislike for children does not become full-blown because of some of the sentimental touches of the director and scriptwriters. Nevertheless, at one point, when asked if he likes children, he replies, "I do if they're properly cooked." This line, along with variations of it, became one of those statements most often quoted.

One of his staples of later pictures, comedy of frustration—more developed when he plays the harassed husband—evolves when Fields is shown trying to mix paint by listening to directions from a "how to do it" radio programme. Naturally, he gets behind the announcer and ends up throwing paint ingredients encased in cans and bags, plus a pet duck that happens to get in the way.

In the picture also appears Fields's tendency to skirt the rigid censorship of the time by using expletives that are substitutes for a strong oath. "Godfrey Daniel!" for example, appears in a way to create colour in his character. When he describes a paddle-wheel ferry boat, he cleans up a remark men have used to describe a woman with a good figure: "She's solid as a brick telephone booth."

A much tighter work than films that were conceived and authored by the comedian, *Tillie and Gus* does not fully capture the spectrum of Fieldsian wit. Mere clean-cut plot lines do not make a W. C. film and in some ways may be too restrictive to exercise the range of his talents. Most important of all, the touches of anti-sentimental character attitude and situations are too few in number. In fact, there are too many sentimental aspects to the leading figures, Tillie and Gus. They end by helping the niece, her husband, and the offspring (Baby LeRoy) to gain their victory over a villainous lawyer named Phineas Pratt (played by the raspy-voiced, wizened Clarence Wilson). As a Mr. Fixit, Fields also loses one of the essentials of his humour—comic frustration. He becomes funnier when *he* gets into a mess, an altercation, or a minor frustrating task. We also find him funnier when he growls his disdain for anything which the dewy-eyed dote upon. We love him when he declares that he hates a child or dog. Now that we've seen this side of his character, we seem to see a false note at the end of the picture when we spy Uncle Gus crawling on the floor before Baby LeRoy, with the pet duck on his back. When his nephew remarks that the ferryboat race was the "world's greatest gamble," the comedian redeems himself somewhat by replying, "No. Don't forget Lady Godiva put everything she had on a horse."

The year 1934 was Fields's most productive period. While it would seem impossible to create one good picture with an output of five pictures that year, the comedian created three strong works. The two he authored, *The Old-Fashioned Way* and *It's a Gift,* were among the best. He reached a new high in the creation of the con-man in the former picture. The fascinating, self-proclaimed "The Great McGonigle" developed into his most interesting version of this type of character to that date. Leader of an itinerant, seedy, theatrical troupe, McGonigle strikes a pose of fame and fortune and becomes comic to the viewer of the film drama when his false pretensions are realised. At the beginning of the picture his character is established when a process server stands with a summons held behind his back as McGonigle starts to board a train. Unnoticed, the crafty impressario lights the official document. As the paper is quickly thrust into his face, it bursts into flame. With great dignity Fields lights his cigar from the rapidly consumed summons; calmly and politely he says, "thank you very much" and boards the train before the startled town official.

From this opening move McGonigle proceeds to work his con-game on all around him. While he is not always successful, he generally wins by some unusual tactic that might be described as comic ingenuity. His brashness and ability to manipulate become the side of his character that promotes the bulk of the humour in *The Old-Fashioned Way.* But other facets still lie beneath the surface to give the character dimension. While he is often on top, he still remains the pretender and the fake who will be crushed in a forthcoming situation. His dignity will suffer when even his daughter exposes his tricks and gives him a lecture on his behaviour. Even when he plays the harassed husband in other films, the con-man lurks in the shadows. To a stranger who does not know him as the dominated husband, he will spin tall tales of his accomplishments as a fighter and adventurer.

Uneven as *The Old-Fashioned Way* is, it remains Fields's first solid creation. It is easy to agree with Andre Sennwald, writing in the "New York Times" of July 14, 1934, that the old-fashioned melodrama scenes from *The Drunkard* are laboured. These play-within-a-play scenes are not the comedian's meat, and he fails to handle the burlesque effectively even though he instils a great deal of gusto into the character of the villain. By far the most interesting part of the show-within-a-show part of the film is the actor's revelation of his vaudeville background as a juggler. Strictly a *lazzi* scene in the fashion of the *commedia dell' arte* theatre, it is a portion that has nothing to do with the plot; it merely shows some special skill on the part of the comedian. Seldom did he use the skill except by juggling a cane and hat as a character trait. Full blown in this little scene are his skills in juggling cane, hat, balls, and cigar boxes. In his feats he makes "mistakes" that lead to even greater feats of the art. We see where his comic character was born. A little man with pretensions and a sense of dignity trying to do his best even when he meets frustration. His act goes awry, but he carries on nevertheless.

At the end of the film the "pathos" in the little man who carries on creates not just a vaudeville act, but the last situation in the plot of *The Old-Fashioned Way.* It is the parting of the ways with his daughter, who is also engaged in show business. In a dignified yet pathetic pronouncement he tells her, "If you need me financially or otherwise . . ." indicating that he is off to a greater glory and fame before the footlights. The last scene shows him on a streetcorner reduced to selling a cure-all that prevents hoarseness. He gives an elaborate speech with the climactic moment ending in a loss of his voice—miraculously restored by a quick swallow of the remedy he is selling.

While *You're Telling Me,* a re-make of the 1926 silent feature, *So's Your Old Man,* was not written by Fields, it deserves a rank among the top five pictures in which he starred. Released in the spring just before *The Old-Fashioned Way,* this work revealed the actor in the role of the dominated husband and inventor. The earlier scenes are the strongest in the movie. Unfortunately, the refurbished golf routine for the final scene fizzled. As an inventor he revealed a humorous eccentricity, but his struggles with a nagging wife promoted the loudest laughter. It was a brilliant beginning using the material that would create some of the greatest comedy of the Thirties.

Critics and audiences viewing films by Fields today seem to think they have discovered him, and a myth has developed that he wasn't appreciated in his day. Andre Sennwald realised that a significant clique had developed by 1934. He seemed to be a part of the clan when he used labels of "The magnificent Mr. Fields," and "the great man." By this time, with uneven works being produced, Fields had become one of the leading comedians.

In his screen career the bulb-nosed W. C. appeared in over forty films. Six short works, one- or two-reel films, are extant. About eight of his silent features seem to be lost. The majority of his films, it may be conjectured, were mediocre. But in 1934 he may have produced his best work. *It's a Gift* certainly is among the top three features he created. Obviously, he was in control of his material, and director Norman Z. McLeod must have known how to make the best use of the talents of his leading players. *Aficionados* have often thought of Fields's humour centring on the con-man, but while he is still the pretender in this picture, he has many traits of the small town grocery store owner who is badgered by his wife, son, and neighbours. The film is a classic study of comic frustration—a view of the little man struggling against the annoyances produced by a collection of petty people in the average community of the United States.

The comic tone of the family misalliance becomes evident early in the picture as the group gathers for breakfast. Consuming all the sugar without a thought for others, the mouthy, eight-year-old son gets reprimanded by his father. The boy complains: "What's the matter, Pop? Don't you love me anymore?" Ready to strike the brat, Fields as Harold Bissonette harshly declares: "Certainly I love yah." His wife harps, "Don't you touch that child!" Defiantly the reply comes: "He's not goin' to tell me I don't love him."

With his family, however, the hapless father is more often on the receiving end of the abuse. Even in his grocery store he is not king. The most demanding creatures of this town, want the impossible from Harold. One of the best scenes in the film shows the comic protagonist pitted against a blind, partly deaf man called Mr. Muckle. Dark humour abounds as the cranky old fellow runs his cane through the front door window of the store, and refusing to stay seated after he comes in, bumps into displays of china and light bulbs. With his attempt to please his patrons regardless of their disposition, Harold Bissonette cries pitifully, "Sit down, Mr. Muckle, please, Dear," as he tries to wrap a package and satisfy another customer, a surly, dignified member of the community named Jasper Fitchmueller, a man bent on obtaining ten pounds of kumquats in a hurry.

In this struggle to please we see Fields in another dimension of his fabulous talent. We laugh at him, but we also feel sorry for him. Maybe a bit of the famed Chaplin pathos develops in this situation. Actually, he becomes a comic hero, with the blind and deaf Mr. Muckle evolving into a comic villain. Only Fields, as it has been noted by critics, could create a scene of this kind.

The little man has a dream. Wishing to escape from it all, he sells his grocery store in order to buy land in California which he believes has a flourishing orchard of orange trees on it. This leads, of course, to a harangue from his wife—forcing him to sleep on the back porch.

The comedian develops a second outstanding sequence by showing Harold's attempt to get to sleep under a barrage of interruptions. Before his exit to the porch the phone rings at 4:30 in the morning. It's a wrong number, but his wife doesn't believe him:

HAROLD: Somebody called up and wanted to know if this is the Maternity Hospital.
MILDRED: What did you tell them?
HAROLD: I told them "no."
MILDRED: Funny thing they should call you up here at this hour of the night from the Maternity Hospital.
HAROLD: They didn't call me up from the Maternity Hospital. They wanted to know if this *was* the Maternity Hospital.
MILDRED: Oh! Now you change it.

Too tired to be exasperated, Harold sputters and mumbles, trying to convince the suspicious wife, but she merely declares, "Don't make it any worse," and blames him for keeping her awake. Stumbling sleepily to the back porch of a three story housing complex with a constant stream of chatter fading in the background, the comic protagonist now encounters a series of interruptions to his sleep that develops into a sequence which becomes a humorous ode to frustration—the main ingredient of Fields's best movies:

1. Harold lies down on the porch swing only to have it break from its mooring on the ceiling. Just the head end falls, and he is left with head and body slanting downward. His wife complains in the bedroom.
2. Enter a milkman with bottles clinking loudly in his wire carrier; this produces mumbled expletives from Harold. "Please stop playing with sleigh bells," he mutters.
3. A cocoanut is delivered to the floor above. When the milkman leaves, the harassed soul settles down in his uncomfortable, improvised, broken bed only to have the cocoanut roll step by step down several flights. This Chinese torture produces a series of flinches from Harold and culminates in a banging and clattering as the cocoanut rolls into garbage cans, shattering the morning calm.
4. Almost fully awake now, Harold tries to fix the head end of the swing. He's interrupted by a smooth-talking insurance salesman who is searching for a man with the

unlikely name of Karl La Fong. Turning his sales pitch to an unwilling subject, he assures Harold he could give him an annuity by which he could retire for life at ninety. His wife enters and yells, "If you and your friend wish to exchange ribald stories, please take it downstairs." Roaring with indignation, "My friend!?" Harold hurries into the house and returns with a meat cleaver in hand. Though he drives the slicker away, he accidentally receives the final humiliation. Exhausted by the ordeal, he drops the meat cleaver on his foot and emits an agonising whine of pain—a high pitched, inward cry smothered by his injured dignity.

5. Wearily he settles on the porch swing only to have a little boy (played by Baby Le Roy) stuff grapes down a hole in the floor above him and drop them on his head. Sleeping with his mouth open, a grape enters and chokes him. "Shades of Bacchus!" he exclaims. Going up to the third floor to stop the bombardment, he gets accused by the mother of feeding grapes to her offspring.

6. As he nearly goes to sleep again, a girl of about sixteen jumps from step to step with her full weight and hits each landing of the stairs so hard she knocks over garbage cans. From the top floor her mother yells to her about the errand on which the girl's being sent. Loudly they discuss the situation, and Harold mutters that he would like to tell them both where to go. Not only is he accused by these two of disturbing them; his wife berates him for fraternising with women.

7. Lying down, Harold rises to the sound of a squeaky pulley on a clothes line—thinking the sound comes from a rat. He sets a trap for the rodent under his swing. Maddeningly, the sound continues.

8. An Italian vegetable and fruit peddler comes by, hawking his wares. Harold runs into the house and returns with a shot gun. Calling sweetly (but ominously), "Vegetable gentleman?" he keeps his gun levelled to shoot. Not able to locate the offender, he sets the gun down and settles into the swing. The gun explodes, and the whole swing breaks from its mooring and comes crashing down. In a heap and without a pause for reaction, he picks up a fly swatter to strike at some critter that landed with him in the rubble.

Simple as this series of incidents may seem, the comedian makes the most of it. Not only do his utterances of annoyance, his misanthropy to those who plague him, contribute to the humour; there are little, futile gestures of frustration and pained expressions masterfully executed which show the actor at his best. The trials and mock agonies of the little man make this twelve-minute sequence one of the landmarks in film comedy.

Unfortunately, this simple, yet effective, sequence becomes the highlight or climax of the best in the picture. The following complications regarding the trip to California have moments, but they do not surpass what comes before. A comic turn of fortune shows Harold's land to be valuable after all because it is adjacent to the future construction of a race track.

After his first masterpiece of the screen, Fields appeared in two works, *David Copperfield* and *Mississippi,* which added to his stature as a comedian. The latter displayed his talents as the con-man again, with a few notable scenes featuring him as the *braggadocio.* More significant on the ledger, however, was the Dickens film. Though British critics found his accent unacceptable, Americans felt his dialect was suitable to play Micawber. Director George Cukor evidently was able to restrain him from incorporating vaudeville bits into his mannerism, and the comedian created a charming character that was an extension of his con-man. More mellow tones and subtle keying of the comic pretensions built into the character by Dickens gave the performance depth. They proved that at the core of a great comedian lies a "dramatic" actor—that is, one who can interpret a role with serious overtones and nuances. Had he lived into the Fifties and been given the opportunity, Fields might have been able to play a role in a Samuel Beckett drama with the skill similar to that Bert Lahr mustered when he enacted the part of Estragon in *Waiting for Godot.*

With the creation of his third authored picture in 1935, *The Man on the Flying Trapeze,* Fields had his second masterpiece. Like *It's a Gift,* the work was totally controlled by the comedian. The story was developed under the pseudonym of Charles Bogle and had many of the qualities of the 1934 work.

Once more he is pitted against family and relatives. As the harassed husband, Ambrose Wolfinger, he pulls a gun from a drawer to investigate burglars prowling in the basement. When the gun accidentally discharges, his wife screams. In sharp understatement, using half a question with a note of hope he queries: "Oh, I didn't kill you? That's fine." Since he remains the henpecked husband until the end of the film (the inner resentment finally explodes and the sponging relatives are put in their place), much of the best laughter of the picture develops from those situations in which others conspire against his attempts at dignity. This is even more evident than in *It's a Gift.* There are also more mumbled understatements by W. C. than in any of his other films. Many are suppressed, muffled comments on his relatives. But there are other incidents that also use this type of wit. Accused of manufacturing apple jack without a permit, he is placed in a jail cell with a madman who has murdered his wife. In a demented frenzy the bug-eyed lunatic confesses, "I had three wives, but this is the first one I have killed in all my life!" Ambrose, with a slight flicker of terror in his eyes, as coolly as possible, observes: "Oh, that's in your favour, yes."

With more understated humour than his other films, *The Man on the Flying Trapeze* becomes an especially delightful work in the Fields gallery of comic portraits. Furthermore, his character in this film exhibits an odd talent that makes him valuable to the business world. A self-proclaimed "memory expert," he can remember trivial incidents which occurred with his boss and his clients. With a perverseness that is comic, he does little paper work and keeps a roll top desk of cluttered correspondence "filed" in a way that only he can decipher.

While *It's a Gift* and *The Man on the Flying Trapeze* have only recently been lauded by critics, *The Bank Dick* (1940) has long been a favourite of *cinephiles*. In content and quality of execution, it certainly can be rated as one of his top three works. The material is clearly linked to similar substance in his two earlier masterpieces. Once more Fields is an author under an odd name—this time the pseudonym is Mahatma Kane Jeeves. All three films feature him in the role of nagged, bumbling, little man living in a small town. Each of these works, while it has imperfections, is dominated by the leading character.

You Can't Cheat an Honest Man (1939), *The Big Broadcast of 1938, My Little Chickadee* (1940), and *Never Give a Sucker an Even Break* (1941), have other comedians whose talents are not as brilliant as Fields's so that the total film meanders in quality of humour and plot. By 1940 reviewers were fully aware of the fact that when W. C. was left to himself as the focus of drama, the work was much better. In the "New York Times" Bosley Crowther held the view that *The Bank Dick* was a superior work because the comedian did not have such "excess baggage as Mae West or even Charlie McCarthy. The picture belongs to him, and his name—or his nom de plume is stamped all over it."

If a person wishes to split hairs, *The Bank Dick* just missed being a product of the Thirties by its release date of 1940. Nevertheless, it was in tone a product of that age that experienced the full range of comedy, and it remains as a masterpiece of its *genre*. Some overlap of the Thirties tradition went into the early Forties. But the World War years were declining years for the comedy, and *The Bank Dick* was the last significant work of the famous comedian.

As in *It's a Gift*, a running gag develops from the last name of the comic protagonist—in *The Bank Dick* the character is called Egbert Sousé. In the former film attempted dignity was stressed through the periodic correcting of people on the French pronunciation of the last name, Bissonette. Built into the name of Sousé is a mispronunciation that reveals a character trait of the protagonist. Naturally, an accent over the "e" becomes necessary to avoid the disparaging label which reveals a comic truth—Egbert practically lives in a bar.

Some of the best scenes of the picture take place in the local saloon and café, the Black Pussy Cat. As the spinner of tales, Egbert explains his exploits in the movies, indicating that he directed Fatty Arbuckle, Chaplin, Keaton,* "and the rest of them." He drawls, "Can't get the celluloid out of my blood." Later, hired as a bank policeman, he grabs a little boy with a cap pistol and asks, "Is that gun loaded?" Angrily the mother replies, "No. But you are." In this film, more than any other, a weakness for drink becomes one of the essential parts of his character. At the end of the drama he seems to have become a successful executive (through the second accidental capture of a bank robber), and his family see him as a changed man whom they now respect. But at the fade-out we see him following the town's bartender who evidently is walking to work to open the Black Pussy Cat.

Another interesting feature of *The Bank Dick* lies in the comedian-author's increased use of character names that make some comic comment—either an abstract or explicit view on the nature of these characters' personalities. While Fields often had a revealing title as a leading or supporting figure in his films, he never employed as many wacky names as in *The Bank Dick*. Those associated with the banking business were Mr. Skinner, president of the establishment and J. Pinkerton Snoopington, bank examiner. More abstract is the label for a lush of a movie director, A. Pismo Clam, enacted by a comic bit actor, Jack Norton, who always seemed to be the drunk in films of the Thirties. In a similar vein J. Frothingham Waterbury is the name for a con-man. Most literal are the "handles" for the bank robbers—Filthy McNasty and Repulsive Rogan. Fields, it should be noted, followed a practice used by authors throughout history, but the technique was used particularly by playwrights in the Elizabethan, restoration and Eighteenth century theatre.

The last stand and fade out of Fields came in

---

*An "in gag" most people in Hollywood would catch. In the silent period these comedians were their own directors.

1941 with *Never Give a Sucker an Even Break.* The gamut of his humour still exists in this rambling work. Like *The Bank Dick,* it contains a climactic sequence which shows the silent screen heritage still influencing the comic film of the Forties. There is a mad dash to the hospital with a woman Fields believes is about to deliver a baby. More novel than the chase of the bank robber in the former work, this scene includes a tangle with the police and a fire truck. Occasionally, other scenes develop effectively with the support of Franklin Pangborn and Leon Errol, but the work becomes disjointed by the inclusion of musical production numbers featuring Universal's second version (the first, Deanna Durbin) of the sweet, young, light opera soprano, Gloria Jean. These portions of the film, like those in *International House* and *The Big Broadcast of 1938,* seem merely to be tacked on and serve only to slow down the development of a work that would be much better without them.

Some films which need only to be briefly cited are *Poppy* (1936), *The Big Broadcast of 1938, You Can't Cheat an Honest Man* (1939), and *My Little Chickadee* (1940). Fields made only cameo appearances in *Follow the Boys* (1944), *Song of the Open Road* (1944), and *Sensations of 1945.* Some fans of the great comedian may object to the slighting of *My Little Chickadee.* It now achieves much of its recognition from its "camp" qualities. Even though it has many good scenes, it is probably the most overrated work in which the comedian appeared. Since Mae West appears in at least half the footage, doing one of the poorer jobs of her career, the total work suffers. Fields has some good lines, but he has trouble playing with the forceful Miss West. Visually, his uneasiness can be detected. He seems frozen before her and only loosens up when he does a scene with minor players.

The explanation of Fields's genius, I believe, lies a great deal in his ability to combine verbal and visual traits in his comic character. His three masterpieces, *It's a Gift, The Bank Dick, The Man on the Flying Trapeze* (to which might be added the first half of *You're Telling Me*) display this fusion at its best. Along with this evolved a more fully developed comic portrait. And this creation proved to be unique for not only the golden age of sound comedy, the Thirties, but also for the great silent screen comedy of the Twenties. Most prominent in both these ages was the young man with traits of dumbness or *naïveté.* To some extent the fast-talking, stand-up comedians entered the scene to play the young man leading roles in the Thirties, but none of them achieved the stature to make them outstanding artists. As a comic protagonist Bill Fields was the only great actor to play the middle-aged and beyond character with a skill that will place him among the immortals.

When I interviewed Buster Keaton in June, 1965, I asked him if he agreed with my choice of Chaplin, Lloyd, Langdon, and Keaton as the four great comedians of the silent age. In failing health which led to his death on February 1, 1966, he did not understand that my evaluation was confined at that time to the silent age of the Twenties. He protested: "Don't forget Bill Fields." I agreed with him then and I do now, after a thorough examination of his films, that Bill was in the king's row. That is, if the silent and sound eras are combined, Fields certainly ranks above Harry Langdon, whose talent was superior to many others but limited when compared to the master of sound comedy.

Critics today should rate this comedian as the king of the Thirties because of his uniqueness, innovation, and many faceted character. At the core of his personality there is the warmth and charm of a Falstaff even though he snarls and mutters insults. In his weak films the power of his enactment of the role comes through. As with Chaplin, we have begun to associate the man with the character, and when that happens, the artist's works become creations for all seasons—for the ages.

Gus has difficulty with a boat in *Tillie and Gus*.

A strained relationship between a long separated couple in *Tillie and Gus* (1933) played by Alison Skipworth and W. C. Fields.

Costumed for *The Old-Fashioned Way* (1934) as the Great McGonigle.

In *The Old-Fashioned Way* the theatrical troupe arrives at a boarding house.

As Commodore Jackson Fields plays a home made cello in *Mississippi* (1935).

At the fade out McGonigle is reduced to selling medicine on the street corner, *The Old-Fashioned Way.*

In *You Can't Cheat an Honest Man* (1939) as Larson
E. Whipsnade, Fields has trouble paying the help.

Selling tickets Fields gets in a hole, *You Can't Cheat an Honest Man.*

In *The Bank Dick* (1940) Egbert Sousé is afraid the boy's gun is loaded.

Even in the most drastic circumstances, Egbert can
be polite in *The Bank Dick*.

Fields as the lover, Cuthbert J. Twillie and Mae West
as Flower Belle Lee in *My Little Chickadee* (1940).

The parting of ways for Cuthbert and Flower Belle
in *My Little Chickadee*.

A moment of alarm as villain Joseph Calleia accuses
the comic protagonist of cheating at cards in *My
Little Chickadee.*

Fields blows the foam from his soda in *Never Give a Sucker an Even Break* (1941) while Irving Bacon wonders about the sanity of his customer.

Taking the elevator to the plateau top and the location of Mrs. Hemogloben's mansion in *Never Give a Sucker an Even Break*.

In *Never Give a Sucker an Even Break* Fields meets one of the strange inhabitants of Mrs. Hemogloben's domain.

In *Song of the Open Road* (1944) Fields appeared in one of his last pictures. With him in this photo, Jane Powell making her screen *début*.

10
The Fading Laughter

While no one put up a sign "Road Closed" because the bridge from one decade to another had been flooded (the flood might be said to be the war years and the period's sociological climate), something happened to the golden age of sound comedy that is startling when viewed from historical perspective. The year in which the laughter faded seemed to be 1940. That year W. C. Fields crossed the line with one very good and one superior movie—*My Little Chickadee* and *The Bank Dick*. A new breed of comic stars was taking over almost as if there were a transition as marked as the two year shift from the silent to the sound cinema. But this time it was a change in tastes and attitudes that reflected the tensions of the approaching Second World War. A lighter, more frenetic, more desultory, and less laughable film began to fill the gap as the slow artistic demise of Laurel and Hardy, W. C. Fields, and the Marx Brothers became clear. W. C. Fields's *Never Give a Sucker an Even Break* in 1941 was the last ray from the sunset—the golden age of sound comedy became a memory.

The entertainment world, prompted by the public's taste for lighter, fluffier, comic adventures seasoned with many songs, turned to popular radio comedians. Almost a key to this new taste in comedy was Bob Hope and Bing Crosby's *Road to Singapore* (1940). Six "Road" pictures spanned the new age, with the last produced in 1962, *The Road to Hong Kong*.

No longer did the patter of vaudeville humour help shape the comedy of the film. During the late Thirties the radio comedy series had shed much of its vaudeville influence and had developed a style of its own. It was a more intimate, gossipy, and low-keyed line of patter. As for comic situation, humorous feuds developed between come-dians Jack Benny and Fred Allen, Bob Hope and Bing Crosby. All starred on their own radio shows and engaged in sniping at each other from a distance; soon the quartet had created combinations that went to the sixth place—that is, wrangling among them eventually developed six feuds. Periodically, one comedian would do a guest spot on his rival's show, and the game of put-down was face to face—or, to be more correct, voice to voice for the radio audience.

The "Road" pictures of Bob Hope and Bing Crosby had all the intimate charm and defects of radio with the visual element added. Attempts to fill the eye, however, were strained. The team was thrown into some exotic and adventurous setting; then, the plot began its ramble through a series of humorous squabbles over a girl, a break for a song, and a series of asides that amazingly sometimes showed the picture making fun of its own defects. Bob and Bing were engaged in some enterprise, seeking gold or diamonds, performing as musicians or actors, or selling something—the activity that usually entered into the plot since they were depicted as good-hearted con men. Dorothy Lamour often became the object of both men's affections. Since Crosby played straight man to Hope, he usually got the girl. As fall guy, Hope more often got into comic hot water, but he usually dragged Bing in with him.

Very disjointed in structure, these comedies show the influence of the radio variety show. All three principals engage in banter that has a ring of radio, not vaudeville. Each gets a chance at a song or two; within the hour and a half running time of a "Road" picture five or six songs are used. In a type of theatricalism that seldom works in the cinema, Bob or Bing direct an aside to the movie audience. Camping in the jungles in *Road* to Zanzibar (1941), Bing jokingly tells Dorothy Lamour that movies often have a man singing to a girl, and regardless of where they may be, an orchestra accompanies him. Bing sings "Always You" and, of course, the strains of a full orchestra come from nowhere. Many gags of this kind in the "Road" films now seem self-consciously cute. As in Road to Zanzibar, gags were often far-fetched. When the two men, working for passage back to America, get tied up with two women in a vaudeville enterprise, they create a magician's routine of sawing a woman in half:

> BING: You sure you know how to do this?
> BOB: (Starting to saw) If not, one of us will go back half fare.

And, that gag was the curtain joke—the humour that topped the whole picture. Probably, the audiences in 1941 were uncritical of this radio-like comedy film and were easily moved to laughter. Today, however, the taste in humour has changed considerably, and such gags only produce groans. The "Road" pictures probably produced little laughter even then. There is a pedestrian feebleness in the comedy; it is more on the level of joshing—a feud with a friend, which reflected the influence of radio comedy.

By himself Bob Hope fared better in his films of the Fifties. Casanova's Big Night (1954) was probably one of his most amusing pictures. As in some of the "Road" movies, he was funny when he registered fear in a dangerous situation while still trying to be manly—a mock of heroics. In the 1954 film he also achieved humour by posing as a great lover when he was, in reality, Pippo the tailor. He dons the attire of Casanova and travels by gondola in Venice, viewing the women who swoon as he sings to them. Hope gives his famous one-liner as he observes the situation: "I'm getting to the age where I can only work a canal a day." The double meaning one-line gag was Hope's specialty.

Bob Hope was an example of the breed of comedians who followed on the heels of the golden Thirties. He had much to his credit—a winning personality and a skill in turning a phrase which indicated that he was an excellent stand-up comedian. On radio he probably was more artistically successful than in the movies. His feature-length portrayals were often inconsistent because he would use any clever line that got a laugh, even if it didn't fit the character. In the Sixties his movies began to seem old-fashioned and contrived;

his spark was gone, and a middle-aged Hope didn't have the eagerness of the early portraits by the personality comedian. I'll Take Sweden (1965) and Boy, Did I Get the Wrong Number (1966) are inferior to any of his works in the Forties and Fifties.

Since the burden of war clouded the minds of people after the formal declaration of war on Japan, December 8, 1941, light entertainment in the form of variety shows and musicals flourished. Biographies of famous song writers and entertainers proved to be in fashion. Al Jolson was still around, and in 1940 he added some flavour to Swannee River as Don Ameche struggled to enact the role of Stephen Foster. A slice of nostalgia more directly related to the war years was the patriotic musical autobiography of George M. Cohan, Yankee Doodle Dandy (1942). In the leading role James Cagney proved that he was as engaging a singer, hoofer, and actor as he had been in Footlight Parade (1933). His acting was many notches higher than the average male lead in a musical. But, as in the past, the musical format established in that fertile year, 1933, assured the more laughable comedians a back seat in the production.

As if there were always an eternal return to the past when the world was under stress, the war years developed the least memorable type of film, the revue. The revue was also prominent during the middle of the stock market crash and the painful transition to sound in 1929. During the war years each Hollywood studio created films that incorporated a collection of all its talent. It was also the era of the big bands and radio. Films employed the bands of Bob Crosby, Tommy Dorsey, Xavier Cugat, Benny Goodman, Woody Herman, Harry James, Spike Jones, Freddy Martin, and Glenn Miller to present the music that had the whole nation gaily dancing away their troubles. Each major studio offered the public a potpourri of entertainment, with music furnished by these big bands. Paramount produced Star Spangled Rhythm (1942); United Artists, Stage Door Canteen (1943); Twentieth Century-Fox, The Gang's All Here (1943); and Warner Brothers, Hollywood Canteen (1944). Each studio had stars who ordinarily acted in serious drama, doing vaudeville or radio variety type of routines. Movie audiences marveled at the minimal skills of these actors and actresses. Whether these thespians did their acts well was not important; only the novelty of their attempts was appreciated—that they could do comedy, sing, and dance. Lost in the shuffle were the studios' many comedians, George Jessel, Harpo Marx, Ned Sparks, Edgar Bergen, Billy Gilbert, Hugh Herbert, Franklin Pangborn, Bob Hope, Jerry Colonna, Joe E. Brown, Eddie Cantor, Jack Benny, and Jack Carson. In 1929 the many revues also submerged the efforts of comedians. The variety and scope of the *genre* gave them only a small portion in which to perform. W. C. Fields was a guest star in such monstrosities—*Follow the Boys* and *Song of the Open Road* in 1944 and in *Sensations of 1945*. But few people can remember his contribution to these works or anything about the films themselves.

Many traditional musicals that displayed all the facets of the Thirties *genre* were produced in the Forties. *Ziegfeld Girl* (1941) starring Judy Garland, Hedy Lamarr, and Lana Turner displayed the lavish dance numbers conjured from the imagination of director Busby Berkeley. A bit of nostalgia, focusing on America in the more innocent age of the early 1900's, *Meet Me in St. Louis* (1944), starred Judy Garland and gave director Vincente Minnelli a hit that would make his talents much in demand for other musicals. A musical adaptation of Eugene O'Neill's *Ah, Wilderness* called *Summer Holiday* featured the same type of nostalgia when it appeared after the war years in 1948. A contemporary theme that followed the exploits of sailors on leave was employed in *Anchors Aweigh* (1945) and *On the Town* (1949). Both works starred Frank Sinatra and Gene Kelly. None of the musicals of this period are memorable for their appeal to a person who wants a good laugh.

In a four year period, 1942-1946, many military service comedies of dubious worth were ground out by the movie factories. The first hit of Bud Abbott and Lou Costello was *Buck Privates* (1941) after they had appeared a year earlier in *One Night in the Tropics*. They did two more service pictures, *In the Navy* and *Keep 'Em Flying*, in 1941.

Abbott and Costello were vaudeville stage trained comics who became prominent in the late Thirties. It was a period of decline for burlesque and not the best time for the development of effective talent. While there are fans who find their movies enjoyable, critically their works are only a couple of notches higher in quality than the films of the Three Stooges. By the late Forties Abbott and Costello had sunk to the level of this threesome with "Meet" pictures. The pair got entangled with "Frankenstein," the "Invisible Man," Captain Kidd, the "Keystone Kops," and finally in 1955 they starred in a vehicle called *Abbott and Costello Meet the Mummy*. Their work now may be appreciated by youngsters aged seven to ten, but the trio never produced any outstanding comedies.

A flicker of past greatness began to emerge with a few comedians who became stars in the Forties. Red Skelton, Danny Kaye, Donald O'Connor, Jack Carson, Joan Davis, Betty Hutton and Jerry Lewis enjoyed public acclaim. However, they are seldom classed with the "greats" of comedy. Each represented a revival of some aspects of the more laughable comedy of the silent and sound golden ages.

Red Skelton borrowed more heavily from the past than the other comedians of the Forties and Fifties and appeared to have all the potential for a crown as a king of comedy. His best films were created between 1948 and 1953, from *The Fuller Brush Man* to *The Clown*. Part of Skelton's strength during this period came from his use of Buster Keaton as a gag writer. *A Southern Yankee* (1948) had many Keaton touches, and director Edward Sedgwick controlled Skelton's tendency to overplay a scene or a specific comedy routine. In future years this picture may be considered his best. The comedian becomes frenetic, however, in a re-make of Keaton's *The Cameraman* (1928) entitled *Watch the Birdie* (1950). In this re-hash of the silent screen picture, Skelton has his moments, but anyone acquainted with Keaton's amazing gifts will find the latter day imitator's version ringing false and strained. In acting a scene, Red Skelton, like so many other comedians of the Forties and Fifties, exhibited a self-consciousness that seemed to say, "Look at me; am I not funny?" The old-timers of the golden years avoided ham acting while displaying the grace and the effortlessness of all fine artists. They usually had the uncanny sense to underplay the emotion a notch below the level which would achieve comedy. An observer might think that underplaying had become a lost art in the Forties and Fifties.

Skelton proved that he could restrain himself in *The Clown* (1952) when director Robert Leonard guided him in a sentimental drama of a has-been clown making a comeback through the medium of television. There was an attempt to gain sympathy for the comic protagonist by using a Chaplin-like "pathos" in the playing of many scenes. The film almost made it, but it occasionally lapsed into sentimentality. The key to Skelton's problem, however, began to be more obvious. Try as hard as he could, he still had trouble becoming the character. He always seemed outside the portrait—a radio or night club comedian doing a sketch; a comic who soon would move to another imitation, a caricature of a person done by some other actor.

Danny Kaye suffered the same malady as Skelton. Displaying all the negative facets of a "naturally born ham," he had the potential to be a great comedian if some director could keep him tethered. His frenetic, unstoppable, driving, pouncing, acting style often became tedious and annoying. His singing and dancing abilities were not used to best advantage since they were injected into so many of his films in a way that interrupted the flow of the action. He needed a director to tell him to cut a routine short before it went beyond the time limit of an audience's appreciation. Nevertheless, Kaye has excellent touches in many of his films. He was well cast in his roles for *The Secret Life of Walter Mitty* (1947), *The Inspector General* (1949), and *Hans Christian Andersen* (1952). Like Skelton he did a re-make of one of the comedy king's films. One of his best works, *The Kid from Brooklyn* (1946) was a refurbished version of Harold Lloyd's *The Milky Way* (1936). His version, like Skelton's, suffers when compared with the creation of a more gifted comedian.

Danny Kaye (as well as Skelton) became a popular comedian on television in the Sixties, and since he usually used a variety show format, he probably felt more at home in this medium. A full length comedy drama tests the metal of any actor. By 1963 Kaye's *The Man from the Diner's Club* compounded all his weaknesses. In this film the comedian occasionally got a laugh without straining, but the overall picture was merely a poor imitation of the older, more effective comedy of the Twenties and Thirties.

As a child actor of thirteen Donald O'Connor first appeared in a feature, *Sing You Sinners,* in 1938. In the Forties and Fifties he became an important comedy star. He received wide public acceptance for the trivial "Francis" series in the Fifties. Francis was a mule that could talk (Chill Wills provided the voice) and was enough of a novelty to be carried into television by its director, Arthur Lubin, under the title "Mr. Ed." This time around, the comic fantasy focused on a talking horse called Mr. Ed. As with most farcical fantasy, there was a built-in pitfall for the actor. More attention was given to the mule (or horse) so

that the leading actor had to play straight man to an animal.

O'Connor, like so many comedians of the Forties and Fifties, was an enthusiastic actor whose charmed workmanship can be admired. But when we look at these films today, we feel cheated; one Donald O'Connor comedy portrait seems to blend into another. Now we find that not one of his films has enough distinction to be preserved in the archives of significant comedy films.

One personality comedian with limited talents but a magnetic presence that never seemed to be exploited to his advantage by writers and directors was Jack Carson. Usually he portrayed the beefy side kick of a lead or played a bit or supporting role in a serious movie. In *The Good Humor Man* (1950) he revealed effective control of his acting level as a comic protagonist. Under the strong direction of Lloyd Bacon, Carson proved he had the potential for a comedy crown. But the time was not ripe for a revival of the slapstick tradition; the overall plot of the piece lacks coherence, and the gags employed were warmed-over Lloyd and Keaton.

The lack of good comedy writing and directing may account for the wasted talents of two comediennes, Joan Davis and Betty Hutton. Both used tomboy and even masculine traits as a means of gaining a laugh, but few writers and directors seemed to know how to handle them. Joan Davis was the more gifted of the two women. She and Miss Hutton shared many of the same comedy talents as Patsy Kelly who was still entangled in a man's world of sports with *Ladies' Day* in 1943. Miss Davis, using the assistance of Leon Errol, crashed the man's world of sleuthing in *She Gets Her Man* (1945). Betty Hutton too often manically mugged her way through a comic routine or song in a musical. What she needed was a director who could control her. Under Preston Sturges's hand she worked effectively with Eddie Bracken in the 1944 *Miracle of Morgan's Creek.*

Of the several comedians of the Forties and Fifties who needed a director and scriptwriter, Jerry Lewis became the prime example of that need. In the Sixties he had attained sufficient status to produce, direct, and star in his own films. By some quirk of modern evaluation and taste, the antics of Lewis now have captivated European critics (particularly in France), and the comedian has been hailed as a superior talent of our time and even a rival of the kings of cinematic comedy. True, his films say something about our society, and occasionally there are scenes of cleverly executed gags and routines. But, in viewing Lewis's total output and examining each film in detail, it becomes apparent that he too often misfires in executing a routine. He often overplays a scene or repeats himself to the point of boring any sensitive member of an audience who has witnessed the best American comedy offered in the Twenties and Thirties.

Jerry Lewis did his best work in his earlier films, *At War with the Army* (1951), *The Stooge* (1953), and *The Caddy* (1953). In the early Fifties he played the dimwitted young friend of Dean Martin's suave, egocentric, and exploitive playboy. This relation was actually a milder, more plausible, and more acceptable version of that link between Abbott and Costello. There was even an attempt to achieve sympathy with a Chaplin-like "pathos" in Lewis's character in *The Stooge*. The sentiment and slapstick didn't always blend effectively in this film, but in *Rock-a-Bye Baby* (1958) these elements clashed. From a creature who was close to idiocy when he tried to mother triplets, Jerry slipped into a likable moron when he sang a love ballad to Connie Stevens.

When Lewis became a solo comedian in the Fifties, he began to slide. In 1960 Gore Vidal's witty stage play, *Visit to a Small Planet* was rewritten for the screen and transformed into a thin slapstick farce geared to the twelve-year-old mind. The comedian completely inverted the urbane, subtle acting style used by Cyril Richard in the stage version. That same year Lewis became producer, scriptwriter, and director of *The Bell Boy*. While Chaplin, Lloyd, and Keaton had the talents to handle their productions from start to finish, Lewis did not. The outstanding comedians of the Thirties, W. C. Fields, Laurel and Hardy, and the Marx Brothers, also had a great deal to say about their productions. They were excellent gag writers and possessed the objectivity and taste to create worthy comedies.

The rich heritage from the stage appeared to have lost its influence in the Forties and Fifties. Stand-up comedians and performers from radio dominated the scene. Even some of the former vaudeville comics like Jack Benny and Fred Allen fared better on radio than they did on the screen. Benny had a few films that were fair, like *To Be or Not to Be* (1942) and *The Horn Blows at Midnight* (1945). Allen was even less successful. His dry delivery and probably the most sophisticated humour ever produced by radio never fully

transferred to films. His visual acting style seemed a bit strained in such works as *We're Not Married* (1952).

In the late Forties British comedy seemed to set a pattern for a new trend. From Ealing studios in London a leading comedian, Alec Guiness, was to capture the attention of the world. An actor with exceptional talent, he played a wide variety of roles in both serious and comic stage plays and films. In *Kind Hearts and Coronets* (1949) he deftly enacted the roles of eight heirs to the Dukedom of Chalfont. With Stanley Holloway he effectively displayed his comic skills in *The Lavender Hill Mob* (1950). Critical attention was turned to Britain, and evaluators gave the many British (mostly Ealing) comedies of the period their blessing, while often looking upon the American scene as too erratic and juvenile to be worthy of attention.

Fortunately, one of the most captivating types of comedy created in the Thirties still existed to a degree during the Forties. William Powell and Myrna Loy, well known for the witty "Thin Man" series, appeared in a Jack Conway directed film, *Love Crazy* in 1941. Powell feigned lunacy in this wacky show to avoid the continuance of divorce proceedings and even engaged in a female impersonation (à la *Charley's Aunt*, the 1892 stage play) by disguising himself as his middle-aged, maiden sister from Saskatchewan. Powell admirably handled the leading role in playwright-director George S. Kaufman's film *The Senator Was Indiscreet* (1947), a brilliant comic expose of a bungling, senile politician. The sophisticated comedy was not dead in the Forties.

Preston Sturges helped to keep the screwball comedy alive. An outstanding screenwriter of the Thirties, he scripted the excellent *Easy Living* (1937) for director Mitchell Leisen. As a director-writer in the Forties he produced his first strong work in *The Lady Eve* (1941). It reflected all the virtues of the past decade's madcap comedy which had its greatest vogue between 1934 and 1938. As in the earlier works, the woman becomes the equal or superior of man. The "Eve" of this comedy eventually gets the best of the man, the "Adam" of the entanglement. The eccentric nature of this couple, played by Barbara Stanwyck and Henry Fonda, becomes evident at the beginning of the show when we see the woman as a con artist who wants to cheat a brewery heir out of his fortune. The rich young man has a hobby of studying snakes and devotes his time to a book called *Are*

Snakes Necessary? As in its heyday during the Thirties, the screwball comedy threw left hooks and many strong uppercuts on the chin of society. Sturges's 1941 *Sullivan's Travels* took a poke at Hollywood's social message directors. His 1944 productions, *The Miracle of Morgan's Creek* and *Hail the Conquering Hero*, were works which had as their targets small town morality and a patriot's fondness for manufacturing and worshipping war heroes. Ernst Lubitsch's European type of comedy showed some of the skill of *Trouble in Paradise* (1932) carried over into the sophisticated comedies *To Be or Not To Be* (1941) and *Heaven Can Wait* (1943). These works and Sturges's were probably too light to be described as satires, but they are a credit to the decade and indicate that one of the most worthy products of the past had continued its influence into an age that witnessed a period of fading laughter.

The heritage of the Thirties exists today in its finest form in the actual works of that decade. In picking the best of the sophisticated or screwball comedies, I would choose *Twentieth Century* (1934) and *Nothing Sacred* (1937). To represent the best in the genteel tradition, *Min and Bill* (1931), *David Harum* (1934), *Ruggles of Red Gap* (1935), and *You Can't Take It with You*

(1938) would have to be included. The musical comedy presents more difficulties, but whatever critical acumen I possess must lean toward *Footlight Parade* (1933), Eddie Cantor's *Roman Scandals* (1933), and *The Wizard of Oz* (1939). This is, of course, considering these works as musical *comedies* with the stress on humour.

A value judgement on the major comedians of the period will place a critic in hot water with fans of Laurel and Hardy, the Marx Brothers, and W. C. Fields. Nevertheless, I find Laurel and Hardy's *Sons of the Desert* (1934), the Marx Brothers' *Duck Soup* (1933), and W. C. Fields's *It's a Gift* (1934) the best work of the masters of sound comedy. As a runner up Joe E. Brown's *Earthworm Tractors* (1936) helps represent one of the best of the minor league comics.

It is possible that there will be a renaissance of film comedy that is as strong as that of the Twenties and Thirties. With present interest in these periods more of the old films are being shown on television, before film societies, and even in the commercial movie houses. The influence is apt to breed imitation, but hopefully, comedians will follow the example of Jacques Tati and Pierre Etaix by adapting the older traditions to their own personalities and styles.

Bob Hope and Bing Crosby in the first of their "Road" pictures, *Road to Singapore* (1940).

Bob Hope on his own in *Son of Paleface* (1952).

The last of the series, *The Road to Hong Kong* (1962), Bing and Bob in international and interplanetary intrigue.

In the 1940 *Swanee River* Al Jolson sings again.

In the final production number of *Yankee Doodle Dandy* (1942), leads (in front) Jeanne Cagney, James Cagney, Joan Leslie, Walter Huston, and Rosemary De Camp.

In *Ziegfeld Girl* (1941) director Busby Berkeley continues to create spectacular dance numbers.

In the front row, Lana Turner, Hedy Lamarr, and Judy Garland, *Ziegfeld Girl*.

Trouble with a street carnival owner (William David-
son), Lou Costello and Bud Abbott in *Keep 'Em Flying* (1941).

Red Skelton plagued by too many girls in one of
his earlier films.

An attempt at Chaplinesque "pathos" in *The Clown*
(1953) with Tim Considine.

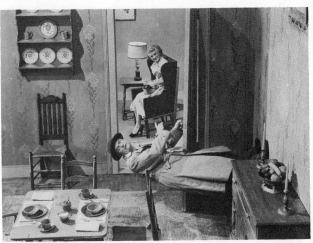

In *The Secret Life of Walter Mitty*, Danny Kaye as Walter has his own fantasy world.

A TV sketch in *The Clown* showing using a surrealistic gag on a hangover.

Kids and dogs love Jack Carson in *The Good Humor Man* (1950).

For *She Gets Her Man* (1945) a publicity still of Joan Davis and Leon Errol.

Patsy Kelly with Max Baer in *Ladies' Day* (1943).

At War with the Army (1950), Dean Martin and Jerry Lewis (far left).

Jack Benny, a star of radio with limited success in films.

Radio comedian Fred Allen with Ginger Rogers in the 1952 *We're Not Married.*

Sterling performances by Stanley Holloway and Alec Guinness made *The Lavender Hill Mob* (1951) one of the best comedies of the time.

Involved with a former flame (Gail Patrick), William Powell has his problems in *Love Crazy* (1941).

Director Ernst Lubitsch's 1943 *Heaven Can Wait* helped to keep the sophisticated comedy alive. From the left, Eugene Pallette, Marjorie Main, Allyn Joslyn, and Charles Coburn.

Peter Sellers (with Capucine) helps carrying on the past tradition of comedy in the 1963 *The Pink Panther*.

In *Shot in the Dark* (1964) Sellers creates effective laughs as Inspector Jacques Clouseau, a bungling detective whose attempts at dignity make the portrait unique.

Selected Bibliography

This annotated list of books does not pretend to be a thorough representation of the many works that have been published on the comedy film. It will, however, provide a guide for the reader who has read *The Golden Age of Sound Comedy* and wishes to continue his investigation of the fascinating world of the comic cinema.

Barr, Charles. *Laurel and Hardy*. Berkeley, California: University of California Press, 1968.

One of the best studies of the comedians. It ranks with William Everson's evaluation in its detailed analyses of the films.

Blesh, Rudi. *Keaton*. New York: Macmillan, 1966.

A solid, accurate view of the comedian's life and works. His talkie career examined in chapters 32 through 38, pp. 314–370.

Brown, Joe E. and Ralph Hancock. *Laughter's Is a Wonderful Thing*. New York: A. S. Barnes, 1956.

Half of this autobiography is concerned with the comedian's stage career. Brown's movie work receives attention when he entered films in the late Twenties (starting on page 174).

Cahn, William. *Harold Lloyd's World of Comedy*. New York: Duell, Sloan, and Pearce, 1964.

A somewhat sketchy account with two chapters (8 and 9) devoted to sound films. Best aspect of this book is Cahn's liberal quotes from interviews with Lloyd which reveal the actor's working methods, comic theories, and views on the work of other comedians.

Cantor, Eddie and David Freedman. *My Life Is in Your Hands*. New York: Blue Ribbon Books, 1932.

A witty, anecdotal account which concentrates on Cantor's stage career. A collector's item that may be difficult to obtain.

Capra, Frank. *The Name above the Title*. New York: Macmillan, 1971.

Many interesting accounts of his life and work in the Twenties and Thirties make this book an important work for the fan and student of cinema.

Baxter, John. *Hollywood in the Thirties*. London: A. Zwemmer, and New York: A. S. Barnes, 1968.

By concentrating on the major studios and directors of the period, this study gives the reader an overall view of the industry in its development of the sound film.

Chaplin, Charles. *My Autobiography*. London: Bodley Head, 1964.

Personal reflections by Chaplin make interesting reading, but he shows less concern for his own working methods than he did in several articles he authored in the 1910's.

Deschner, Donald. *The Films of W. C. Fields*. New York: Citadel Press, 1966.

Created during the flood of picture books in the Sixties, this work provides effective data on Fields's films with excerpts from contemporary reviews.

Dressler, Marie and Mildred Harrington. *My Own Story*. Boston, Mass.: Little and Brown, 1934.

Final chapters, 15 through 18, deal with Miss Dressler's film career in the early Thirties. Most of her autobiography is concerned with her stage career.

Durgnat, Raymond. *The Crazy Mirror; Hollywood Comedy and the American Image*. London: Faber and Faber, 1969.

An attempt (not always very successful) to evaluate by sociological means the history of comedy films in the U.S.

Everson, William K. *The Art of W. C. Fields*. Indianapolis, Indiana: Bobbs-Merrill, 1967.

An excellent analysis of the actor's work with only minor lapses in accurately recording the dialogue of his pictures. It is superior to Taylor's study.

———. *The Films of Laurel and Hardy*. New York: Cadillac, 1967.

Everson knows his subject and does a thorough job of analysing all of the team's films.

Eyles, Allen. *The Marx Brothers; Their World of Comedy*. London: A. Zwemmer, and New Jersey: A. S. Barnes, 1966.

By far the best evaluation of this comedy team's movies with only occasional lapses in accuracy in quoting the dialogue used in specific films. Good data in the appendices.

Fowler, Gene. *Schnozzola; The Story of Jimmy Durante.* New York: Viking Press, 1951.

A highly entertaining account, but the famous biographer of Mack Sennett and John Barrymore uses elaborate conversations that must be interpolations and the fancy of the author.

Keaton, Buster and Charles Samuels. *My Wonderful World of Slapstick.* Garden City, New York: Doubleday, 1960.

The sound films of Keaton are discussed from chapter 12 through 15, pp. 219–282. Some interesting views on his working methods make this autobiography very important.

Hecht, Ben. *A Child of the Century.* New York: New American Library, 1954.

A witty autobiography of one of Hollywood's most prolific and literate screenwrights who assisted in the development of the sophisticated comedy in the Thirties.

Huff, Theodore. *Charlie Chaplin.* New York: Henry Schuman, 1951.

A thorough, detailed study of the life and works of the famous comedian. One of the best evaluations of Chaplin.

Lahr, John. *Notes on a Cowardly Lion; The Biography of Bert Lahr.* New York: Alfred A. Knopf, 1969.

The son of comedian Lahr probably should have left his task to someone else; nevertheless, the evaluator has gathered some effective details on the comedian's career and attempts to explain his father's relatively unsuccessful bout with the film medium.

Maltin, Leonard. *Movie Comedy Teams.* New York: New American Library, 1970.

A worthy, fascinating study of many major and minor comedy duos plus trios such as the Marx Brothers, the Ritz Brothers, and the Three Stooges. Filmographies that are included are excellent.

Marx, Groucho. *The Groucho Letters; Letters from and to Groucho Marx.* New York: Simon and Schuster, 1967.

Provides more evidence that Groucho is a very clever man and shows his relationship with a wide range of individuals who seem also to enjoy the act of corresponding with the famous comedian.

———. *Groucho and Me.* New York: Dell, 1960.

While this autobiography does not concentrate enough on the comedian's work in the movies, it is a must for fans of his wit.

Marx, Harpo and Rowland Barber. *Harpo Speaks!* New York: Bernard Geis, 1961.

Insights into Harpo's evolutionary creation of his clown character make this work valuable. Harpo often seems more concerned with his associations with famous literary and entertainment personalities.

McCabe, John. *Mr. Laurel and Mr. Hardy.* Garden City, New York: Doubleday, 1961.

McCabe's affectionate grasp of this team's comedy makes this study worth reading, but it should be realised that he often interpolates and jumbles details when he tries to evaluate specific scenes of their films.

McCaffrey, Donald W. *Four Great Comedians; Chaplin, Lloyd, Keaton, Langdon.* London: A. Zwemmer, and New York: A. S. Barnes, 1968.

While this work concentrates on the Twenties, the influence of the silent screen tradition on the sound film is analysed in the final chapter of the book.

——— (ed.). *Focus on Chaplin.* New York: Prentice-Hall, 1971.

A collection of articles by critics and Chaplin himself that covers the comedian's work with Mack Sennett in 1914 to his last important feature, Limelight, *in 1952. Covers the range of critical attitudes and methods of evaluating Chaplin's films.*

McVay, Douglas. *The Musical Film.* London: A. Zwemmer, and New York: A. S. Barnes, 1967.

This evaluator devotes only 22 of his 164 page study to the musical of the Thirties because he views the creations of the Forties, Fifties, and Sixties to be superior.

Montgomery, John. *Comedy Films.* London: George Allen and Unwin, 1954.

While the evaluator may overrate the importance of the British contribution to silent screen comedy, his book provides one of the best overall histories of the genre *by tracing the developments of this type of film from its origin to the early Fifties.*

Platt, Frank C. (ed.). *Great Stars of Hollywood's Golden Age.* New York: New American Library, 1966.

Even though the articles in this collection are often on the level of the impressionistic fan magazine, there are interesting pieces on Carole Lombard, the leading actress of sophisticated comedy, and Charles Chaplin.

Springer, John. *All Talking! All Singing! All Dancing!* New York: Cadillac, 1966.

Basically a picture book, this evaluation is somewhat sketchy and opinionated. But the many stills help capture some of the spirit of the musical and its history since The Jazz Singer *(1927).*

Taylor, Robert Lewis. *W. C. Fields; His Follies and Fortunes.* Garden City, New York: Doubleday, 1949.

Interesting reading is provided by this study which

sometimes is marred by gross distortions when detailed analyses are attempted—for example an account of The Bank Dick, *pp. 326–333. The author fortunately confines most of his efforts to the life of Fields.*

Twomey, Alfred E. and Arthur F. McClure. *The Versatiles: A Study of Supporting Character Actors and Actresses in the American Motion Picture, 1930–1955.* New York: A. S. Barnes, and London: Thomas Yoseloff, 1969.

Data and pictures of 600 film players, many of them important contributors to the effectiveness of the Thirties comedy film.

Vallance, Tom. *The American Musical.* London: A. Zwemmer, and New York: A. S. Barnes, 1970.

For the critic and film buff this book contains a wealth of data on the genre *with discussions under such classifications as "Band Leaders," "Composers on the Screen," "Ghosting," etc.*

Vreeland, Frank. *Foremost Films of 1938; A Yearbook of the American Screen.* New York: Pitman, 1939.

Unfortunately this rare book can only be found in a few libraries and private collections. Contains absorbing views on trends in film comedy and detailed analyses of Love Finds Andy Hardy, Snow White and the Seven Dwarfs, *and* You Can't Take It with You. *A pioneer effort in the study of the popular cinema.*

Zimmerman, Paul D. and Burt Goldblatt. *The Marx Brothers at the Movies.* New York: New American Library, 1970.

Originally published as a hardback by G. P. Putnam's Sons in 1968, this work seems to be indebted to Allen Eyles's study. Good use of illustrations with the text.

Index of Names

Index of Films